# Cultural Affairs
# and
# Foreign Relations

WASHINGTON, D. C.

COLUMBIA BOOKS, PUBLISHERS

1 9 6 8

# Table of Contents

# Preface

The American Assembly published the first edition of this volume, edited by the late Robert Blum, as preparatory background for the Twenty-second American Assembly held at Arden House in October, 1962. It served the same purpose for nine subsequent local and regional meetings and for the first Asian-American Assembly held at Kuala Lumpur, Malaysia in 1963. It has enjoyed a wide circulation, and the present thorough revision and expansion is published to meet a continuing demand.

Two essays appear here for the first time, written by C. Easton Rothwell and by Kenneth W. Thompson. They replace chapters of the earlier edition on similar topics. The other three essays have been altered to take account of developments of thought and program during the past six years. They are as relevant as when first written, perhaps more so. The authors of these essays have joined to gather insights from the experience of past United States involvement in cultural activities, to illuminate unmet opportunities, and to stimulate and urge farsighted policy review and fresh commitment by all concerned. Their views are their own and not those of The American Assembly, which takes no position on matters it presents for public discussion.

The American Assembly program on Cultural Affairs and Foreign Relations was originally supported by a grant from The Hazen Foundation and The Danforth Foundation equally. The present edition of this volume was made possible by the generosity of the Laurel Foundation.

Clifford C. Nelson  
*President*  
The American Assembly

January, 1968

iv

*PAUL J. BRAISTED, Editor*

# Introduction

## Toward A More Humane World

Cultural affairs arise from man's unending search for understanding of the world and himself. Culture contact and culture change are aspects of a common human experience. Fresh encounter with a vigorous and unfamiliar culture has often been the means of revolutionary flowering of a new cultural experience. Japan's eager acceptance of the culture of Tang China in the ninth century and the western scientific democratic civilization in the nineteenth century mark two periods of remarkable cultural development. Although China developed for long centuries in isolation from and ignorance of important cultural developments in other and distant parts of the world, her nineteenth century encounter with the Western world was the beginning of her continuing march toward modernization. Today varied cultural contacts of peoples in all parts of the world are more complex, intensive and influential—both for good or ill—than ever before. The primary purpose of this series of essays is to refocus attention upon the essential nature of cultural relations, the recent experience of the United States in relation to the unprecedented opportunities of the present and near future, and the principles of wise national policy in the emerging world society.

## The Nature of Cultural Affairs

The age-old flow of ideas and people has been greatly enhanced in recent times. This development is the result of ever-accelerating scientific and technological advances, the improvement and far-extension of education at all levels, and the rapid expansion of transportation and communications. It is both enriched and confused by the emergence of many new nation states. It is shaped to an important degree by the tension and clash of new ideologies in the midst of still vigorous traditions. The number, scope and complexity of these emerging and ever-changing situations and the problems and opportunities they create would have been unimaginable even a few years ago.

The term "culture," deriving from its agricultural roots, has been used in various ways—such as the refinement of arts and letters of French *culture*, the evolutionary *Kultur* of the German tradition, as well as the modern sociological and anthropological use of the term suggested above. The essays in this volume are primarily concerned with culture as science and technology, education, the arts and the humanities. Since no modern nation can be indifferent to these matters, the authors are concerned with the development of wise national and international policies. Their thought is developed in the broad, comprehensive and universal perspective of history and humanity. Thus George Shuster develops "a theory of cultural relations," with a world perspective including a review of the United States experience in cultural relations. Likewise other writers provide numerous illustrations of international cooperation such as the international geophysical year, programs of educational, economic or technological aid and exchanges of art and books, artists, musicians, dramatists and others. Although these activities are of recent origin, fragmentary and subject to alien currents of contemporary strife, they point toward the possible emergence of an unprecedented, rich and full cultural experience for all men.

Cultural activities are handicapped by enormous obstacles. There are ancient traditions, deep-rooted and tenacious, which yield only slowly to the rising demands of people for a share in a richer, modern life. Nation states, large and small, jealously guard their sovereignty, often in absolute forms, and seemingly are as yet unable to join in creating a world community. Meanwhile the increase of population, in large measure the result of the conquest of disease and improvement in health, raises a spectre of unprecedented upheaval, hunger and pestilence. But these and other obstacles are not of the order of natural phenomena and disasters. They are mainly the creations of men at varying times in history and, as such, may be modified by the imaginative use of human intelligence. It is surely one of the most significant features of these times that these obstacles are being attacked, as never before, through cooperation in education, exchanges of persons and the acquisition of scientific and other knowledge.

It is perhaps natural that in the environment of turmoil in all continents in an age of swift change, public attention tends to focus upon current crises. But change always holds the possibility of initiative and improvement in the human situation. It is part of the intention of this book to urge greater concentration upon exploiting opportunities for cultural development which, begun even now, will extend far beyond the clamor and tumult of present conflicts.

The nature and vitality of cultural affairs is described and illustrated in a variety of ways by the essays which follow. Thus, George Shuster recounts the history of the debates and practices of the recent decades. McNeil Lowry and Gertrude Hooker, in the context of a description of purposes of exchanges in the musical arts, theatre, drama, ballet and the visual arts, direct attention to current unsolved problems and unmet opportunities. Easton Rothwell develops a new statement of a theory of education in relation to cultural relations of nations and peoples, illuminates this with recent history and points out the newly emergent opportunities for cooperative work. Roger Revelle, in the framework of search for understanding of the world and the use of such knowledge, focuses attention upon international cooperation in science and in technical assistance. The diffusion of scientific knowledge, the interdependence of nations, the interpenetration of the ambitions and frustrations of the peoples of the world show that the exchanges of people and ideas, of learning and of information, are of primary importance to modern man. From this arises an urgent need for citizens of the United States and the West generally to understand their own values better and, therefore, the possible relevance of them to other peoples caught in the cross currents of transition from traditional to modern ways of life. Likewise, they need to gain a deeper understanding both of the traditional culture of the peoples of the Middle East, Africa, Asia and

Latin America, as well as their varied situations in the contemporary and emerging cultural world. In these ways we
will surely gain much enrichment for our own life, but may
find new and more sophisticated ways to assist in the cultural development of other peoples.

## SOME ELEMENTS OF WISE NATIONAL POLICY

This is not the occasion for recounting the long and
exceedingly varied history of the participation of Americans
in the worldwide flow of cultural activities and exchanges.
Rather attention is focused upon the development of United
States policies and programs of the past two or three decades. One of the perennial problems has been how to
develop closer relations both among universities and other
cultural institutions on the one hand, and the numerous
interested government agencies on the other. The fact that,
in spite of newly developed cooperative efforts, there remains an almost instinctive resistance to "coordination,"
suggests that a primary need is for imaginative invention of
more effective means of cooperation. There is a felt need
for, and indeed on occasion a continuing search for, better
management and avoidance of duplication of efforts. The
very substantial increase in the number of people professionally engaged in the development of international cultural programs makes problems of relationships more
urgent and frequently critical. There are other practical
matters suggested by McNeil Lowry and Gertrude Hooker,
such as the need for provision of long term rather than
annual governmental support and scrupulous avoidance by
government of any confusion of cultural activities with
short range "information programs"—points further developed in *The Neglected Aspect of Foreign Affairs* by Charles
Frankel. These problems involve both legislative and administrative arrangements for government support of intercultural activities. A deeper understanding of the social and
cultural world environment is essential to the success of
national political and economic policies.

This understanding is particularly urgent and essential
for the thinking and action of all government leaders at all
levels. It is especially acute in any educational or economic
aid programs which can arouse, on occasion, misunder-

standing, disdain or bitterness when not imaginatively related to particular cultural situations. From another angle one must recognize the political atmosphere which at times becomes highly charged and which increasingly involves not only the great powers, but all nations as well. The most acute danger is that short range political concerns may not only interrupt cultural programs, but by compromising their integrity and their essentially humane nature, deny their full creative impact on the future.

It is not too much to say that the brightest hope for mankind exists wherever free institutions and free spirits maintain their clear vision and conduct their affairs independent of the narrow proximate aims of tradition, state or block of states. In contemporary society cultural affairs are inextricably involved in the relations of states to one another, whether unilaterally or in and through international agencies. Such endeavors are often the means to great good in the improvement of food production, increase in public health, the extension of educational opportunities and in technological development. Such good may derive from direct government programs, as well as from the initiative of individuals and cultural agencies, but they reach their greatest potential where, as in the International Geophysical Year, or in some programs of UNESCO, they reflect genuine uninhibited cooperation and stimulate the efforts of numerous government and private agencies as well as individuals among and within the countries concerned. Governments may also encourage free institutions such as universities, institutes, foundations and individual scholars, and from time to time borrow their resources of knowledge and personnel to mutual advantage. But this priceless cultural resource, the proud boast of "open societies," rich and varied in the United States, can be and sometimes is impaired or wasted when, carelessly or intentionally, the autonomy and integrity of free institutions are compromised. Irreparable damage can be done by unreflective, myopic concentration upon immediate political goals or by covert involvement of individuals or institutions in political activities. International relationships are of many kinds, but those in the realm of cultural activity require very careful sensitive understanding and appropriate nurture for their survival and effectiveness. What is too little recognized is the hazard, and need for unflagging vigilance by all concerned, but especially by the free institutions and individuals themselves. Loyalty to the human treasure of culture requires dedication not only to its preservation, but also to its increase everywhere throughout the world. Thus governments and free institutions need not be at counter purposes, but may be mutually helpful, but only when the minds of men and their cultural institutions are indeed free.

The national interest in these times is challenged by the irresistible demands for modern development among peoples in all continents. There exists an unprecedented opportunity for mutually beneficial efforts devoted to the improvement of health, education, economic and social development. Nor is this opportunity limited to the countries considered at a particular moment to be friends and allies. It has been demonstrated that there is mutual advantage in cultural activities, even among rivals, such as that which has developed between the Soviet Union and the United States. This and other indicators, as well as the long history of mutually constructive and advantageous cultural relations with the Chinese people, point to the necessity, at as early a time as possible, of the development of cultural activities with continental China. The national interest also requires a broadening of the cultural perspectives and horizons of Americans at all levels of education. Important and highly significant efforts have already been made to free education from its parochial confines within the Western tradition and to give it a world perspective. But this good beginning has yet to be followed up and developed to its fullest implications.

## THE FUTURE

This volume is primarily concerned with tomorrow. Throughout the descriptions of programs, the discussion of obstacles and the need for change, is the acute awareness of almost unlimited opportunities for enrichment and improvement of the common life of mankind. This is the main theme of Kenneth Thompson in the concluding essay of the volume where, drawing upon the rich and varied experience of the primary agents of cultural activity—universities, foundations and related agencies—he suggests principles for use in the development of wise national policy and program both by the private agencies and especially by government leaders and agencies.

# 1. The Nature and Development of United States Cultural Relations

## GEORGE N. SHUSTER

Cultural relations in the modern sense have a relatively brief but impressive history. The major European colonizing powers, notably France, Germany and Great Britain, increasingly aware of their social responsibilities to the dependent peoples as well as of the reliance which necessarily had to be placed on native civil servants and ruling castes, came at the turn of the century to rely more and more on cultural influence as an instrumentality of cooperation. This experience was later made the basis of policy toward other nations. A remarkable network of services was developed, designed for all levels of education and often particularly concerned with the arts. The results achieved were frequently quite remarkable. Today we are seeing the extent to which all this has been merged with the cultures of the peoples once guided and influenced, but now independent.

One should note also the Christian missionary experience and effort on all continents, most notably Asia and Africa. Schools, medical centers and later on even universities were established, local dialects were transformed into literary languages, and native missioners were recruited. The value of all this to the colonial powers was obvious; and although France itself was governed by laws rigorously separating Church and State, no such policy was adopted in so far as the colonies were concerned. Protestant, later on Catholic, missionary activities sponsored by Church groups in the United States stood in a wholly different relationship to their government. Yet this did in several ways support the work of the missions, and in turn during a good many years relied upon them as major sources of information. Although the character of missionary effort has changed radically since the decline of colonialism the fact remains that it is still a major factor in cultural relations, now particularly in Africa and Latin America.

## THE ORIGINS

It was this development which furnished a spur and indeed a kind of model when during the administration of President Franklin D. Roosevelt what has been familiarly termed the "Good Neighbor Policy" toward Latin America was inaugurated. To be sure, there had been some activity on the part of the United States in the area of cultural exchange prior to July 2, 1938, when a departmental order implementing the "Good Neighbor Policy" created the Division of Cultural Relations in the Department of State. Most of this activity had taken place as a result of private initiative, although the federal government had also been active in a modest way. The Smithsonian Institution had been authorized by the Congress to make provision for the export of literary and scientific materials. The indemnities accruing to this country as a result of the Boxer Rebellion were set aside by agreement with the government of China to assist students from that country. Upon occasion, ambassadors and consuls were to all intents and purposes cultural envoys as well, as witness James Russell Lowell and Nathaniel Hawthorne in an earlier time.

But 1938 was a year of decision in so far as the public policy of the United States in the field of cultural relations is concerned. The subsequent stages in the formation and execution of that policy may be noted:

First, the pioneer efforts of the Division of Cultural Relations.

Second, the blending of cultural activities and propaganda during the war years and thereafter.

Third, the entry of the United States into the area of international cooperation, marked by the establishment of UNESCO in 1945 and 1946.

Fourth, subsequent efforts to insure a climate of mutuality and also to improve the quality of the operation.

We shall review these briefly (Unfortunately there is no treatise which outlines them in desirable detail.), so that the major issues can be discerned and some basis laid for projecting them into the future.

### The Division of Cultural Relations

The Division of Cultural Relations was in many ways a novel undertaking. The staff of the Department and a General Advisory Committee were conjoined in an effort to carry out, on behalf of the United States, the provision of the Convention for the Promotion of Inter-American Cultural Activities, signed in Buenos Aires in 1937. Viewed in retrospect, this was a quite modest program, concerned primarily with the exchange of persons on a scale which now seems diminutive. It is, however, worthy of note that exchanges would continue to remain of vital interest in every cultural relations program to follow. As time went on and war in Europe as well as in the Far East cast its tragic shadow on the world of man, China, Africa, and the Near East were included in the Division's concern. Later on, the Division also took under advisement the problem of how to assist German education in casting off the shackles of Nazism, and participated in planning for the future with the Conference of Ministers of Education in exile. But before much of this thinking could be transformed into some kind of practice the Department of State placed all its eggs in the propagandistic incubator of the Office of War Information.

In several respects, the Division of Cultural Relations established concepts which continue to be central in our thinking. First, the emphasis it placed on the exchange of persons has been retained, though the number of those involved is almost incalculably greater. As a matter of fact, no one may actually know how many people are engaged, for in addition to such Exchange Programs as are sponsored by the Department of State and the Agency for International Development, there are those of the Armed Forces, the National Science Foundation, the Central Intelligence Agency, and other branches of the government.

Second, the Division threshed out in long and sometimes strenuous debates the question as to whether a cultural relations effort should be disinterested in character, or whether it ought openly (or upon occasion covertly) to serve a propagandistic purpose. For obvious reasons, a program which relied solely on the mutual exchange of cultural achievement and experience came to seem to be impractical during the War and cold war years. But, as we shall see, there has been a marked increase recently of support for the idea of having a body of cultural activities in which the national political interest is not directly involved.

Third, when in 1941 the Division established the post of Cultural Relations Officer (later on to be rechristened "Cultural Attaché"), the qualifications were these:

> . . . . they should have a suitable personality that would assure their ability to work effectively with the people of the country in which they may be located; they should have broad intellectual and cultural interests, and should be capable of understanding and appreciating matters of which they may not have specialized knowledge; they should have constructive imagination and enthusiasm; their point of view should be that of a mature, educated person, and they should have good judgment and common sense. It may be assumed that they have a fluent command of the language of the country to which they are sent, but they should be willing to endeavor to learn to use the language with distinction as well as with readiness.

It is perhaps unnecessary to state that very few of our fellow citizens possess the requirements thus outlined. In the first group selected some of them did, as witness Thornton Wilder, Charles Rufus Morey, and Herschell Brickell. But the post was soon downgraded, the number of appointees was nevertheless legion, and some of the results were hair-raising. The United States was in certain instances represented by Cultural Relations Officers who should not have survived the sophomore year in any reputable college. More recently, however, the Department of State has thought of sending abroad at least a limited number of men and women whose qualifications would resemble those insisted upon in the days of yore by the Division of Cultural Relations.

Fourth, the General Advisory Committee, by reason of its interest in Latin America and the Near East in particular, promoted the idea of establishing American Libraries abroad and concerned itself directly with the then new Benjamin Franklin Library in Mexico City. It also began to consider ways in which American schools and colleges abroad, most of which had come into being on the initiative of missionary bodies, could be assisted by the government. The subsequent development of both these forms of endeavor is one of the notable facts in the history of the cultural relations of the United States.

### The influence of the British Council

But of all the reflections of the time described, no doubt those which had to do with the British Council continue to have the greatest influence, though no comparable institution was established in the United States. Those who are interested in the discussion of this establishment may be referred to *The Cultural Approach,* by Ruth McMurray and Muna Lee. Here we shall merely note that the Council was a departure from normal British diplomatic practice. Though it had government financial support, it was nevertheless an organization of private citizens, many of whom had had years of experience abroad. The idea that the United States government could indirectly support private groups was at that time novel. But it has since become a quite normal procedure. In addition, the example of the British Council very greatly encouraged those who believed that an effective cultural relations program should be divorced from official propaganda.

Perhaps the most easily observable result of studying the activities of the British Council was that the Department of State began as early as 1939 to channel some of its cultural activities through private groups. The Institute of International Education started to serve as the operational agency for exchange grants, and the American Council on Education was active in the same field. Since that time, the number of such arrangements has greatly increased. Indeed, it may not be incorrect to say that one of the major innovations in the procedures of the federal government has been the transfer of operational responsibility for a number of its programs to private or semi-private groups and organizations.

This is the broad outline of the cultural relations policy of the United States until our entry into the Second World War. The titanic struggle was also much more a test of strength between conflicting ideologies than any previous war had been, save perhaps the initial stages of general

European resistance to the French Revolution. The British Council, as a matter of fact, had come into being largely because it was thought necessary to counteract the ruthless propaganda machine of Dr. Goebbels, designed to till fields of the mind and the emotions in all parts of the world. The cold war had begun, though probably no one realized it at the time.

## WAR-TIME PROPAGANDA AND AFTERMATH

The Office of War Information into which the cultural program of the Department of State was absorbed during the Second World War signaled a relatively complete, though presumably temporary, victory for the point of view that propaganda for the democratic philosophy of the United States must always be the true purpose of cultural activities, however discreetly camouflaged it might be. Indeed, this point of view remained dominant in the Congress and elsewhere for a longer time than most observers had perhaps foreseen. It is therefore desirable to put it in some sort of perspective.

### The "American Century"

Wartime needs or the broader desirability of counteracting the vicious though, for many, attractive doctrine of the Nazis, were associated during the early forties with the belief, shared by a brilliant group of historians, political theorists and publicists that the "American Century" lay ahead. This would be a time in which the institutions and basic "philosophy" of the United States would seem so self-evidently right that all men who were capable of sound reason would desire them for their countries. It was therefore imperative that the American people realize their manifest destiny and set about, through a vigorous mission of persuasion, to spread the gospel they had brought to fruition during a century and a half. Here, then, was the obvious answer to the totalitarians like Hitler. Another version of the American Century doctrine was that of the "Anglo-Saxon heritage." For the advocates of this, British and American experience had fused in successfully making a pragmatic demonstration of the superlative value of a free, constitutionally governed society.

Neither of these points of view was ever formally endorsed by the United States government, but very competent writers expounded them in pungent or eloquent prose. There was a good deal which could be said in their favor. But perhaps it was not obvious enough then that if there was to be an "American Century" the demand would have to come from the peoples of the world rather than from our telling them that the course of human destiny was in our hands. It would later on become clear that there was considerable reluctance around the globe to accepting the American Century with glee, especially when some of the salesmen neither knew what their wares were or how to make friends and influence people. Meanwhile the Congress tended to view the matter in the light of how much it was costing and how patriotic the merchandise could be deemed to be.

### Office of War Information and successors

It is not within the scope of this essay to discuss the character or the achievements of the Office of War Information. What needs to be stressed, however, is that the OWI led to the creation of propaganda instruments which would continue to be of great use, however perplexing it might on occasion be to decide on how to employ them. The most impressive of these are the United States Information Agency, its Information Services, and its Voice of America. Both are of importance to the development of our cultural relations policy, for a variety of reasons. The "American Century" idea was at first implicit in both. They were pressed into service after the war to help insure the ideological renovation of Germany and Japan; and though there were marked differences between the methods used in the two countries, the basic common objective was to inculcate respect for, and if possible allegiance to, the democratic way of life. In what manner could this be more satisfactorily or effortlessly attained than through advertising the characteristics and achievements of the United States? The attempt necessarily required a good measure of experimentation, and it also became obvious that differences in social and political outlook would plague those in charge. The Voice of America was therefore often an object of praise, derision, or acceptance with a shrug of the shoulder. The Information Services of USIA fared some-what better though they too sometimes found the going extremely difficult. A careful study of both (which cannot be attempted here) would undoubtedly provide a valuable illustration of the strength and the weakness of nationally sponsored propaganda activities.

The Voice of America was the first attempt made by the federal government to enter the highly important field of radio broadcasting. Several major problems presented themselves and even now have not been solved. First, the divorce between domestic broadcasting and government which is necessary under our laws and traditions made it im-possible to carry over into propaganda or information broad-casting abroad the experience and skills of the great private companies. This was a handicap with which the British Broadcasting Company, for example, being a governmental institution, did not have to reckon. The Voice has accord-ingly always been at least in some measure an enterprise of amateurs. It has unquestionably improved, but the major difficulty encountered likewise by educational radio and television—which is that of adequate competence in script preparation and technical management—still exists today. It cannot be removed by merely increasing the pro-duction know-how.

The challenge now presented by the conquest of space and the resulting feasibility of satellite broadcasting is one which has taxed the ingenuity of our technical experts and our cultural leadership. There is something awesome and indeed frightening in the fact that it is already possible to broadcast to half the world from one place at one time, and that the availability of low-priced transistor receivers will prodigiously increase the number of potential listeners. On the one hand the educational benefits which might result are very great, but on the other the spectre of conflicting waves of propaganda is not to be banned. It would seem well worth considering whether an international consortium to share in the devising of programs of satellite broadcast-ing is conceivable, starting out at first with the peoples of the Western Alliance and then later inviting the cooperation of other peoples. It is also possible to think of regional satellite broadcasting, and some progress toward planning it has been made in Latin America. Unfortunately the accomplishments of private broadcasting in the area of television and radio are too limited in scope to serve as models. There are, for example, the modest efforts of the Broadcasting Foundation of America.

### Libraries and publications

The Information Services of USIA began in much the same way as did the Voice. The seedlings initially planted in international soil by the General Advisory Committee on Cultural Relations, as it set about fostering a small number of schools, libraries and cultural centers, were now distributed in huge bundles, particularly, once more, in Germany and Japan. Newspapers and magazines were created and subsidized. Books were translated or distributed in English. But it was the *Amerikahaus* and its equivalent which made by far the greater impact. At least this was the case in Germany. Considered in the tranquil light of everyday intellectual intercourse, the *Amerikahäuser* were not only depositories for literature bearing the imprint of publishers in the United States but places where those interested, and they were many, could attend lectures, hear concerts, view exhibits of art. If at first the major emphasis was somewhat tiresomely placed on the virtues and good deeds of the United States, they gradually became civilized places in which the universality of culture was respected.

But perhaps the most notable propagandistic purpose served was to demonstrate the friendly and perhaps somewhat lavish manner in which we Americans made reading materials available to the public. One could enter and take from an open shelf books or periodicals which in most parts of Europe were kept behind locked doors and made available only on application. It is of course true that Europeans were not so much being niggardly as making an effort to have the materials in question on hand for all borrowers. American libraries abroad—that in Paris and the Benjamin Franklin Library in Mexico were worthy ancestors of the *Amerikahaus*—are probably among the most effective media through which our culture could be brought to the attention of the world. The "open shelf" principle, to which we have grown so accustomed that we scarcely pay attention to it, is even now something which other nations generally associate with inordinate confidence in the honesty of readers. Yet in some cities today more people read books in the libraries we staff and equip than do so in the similar establishments maintained by the host countries. This is an achievement in which we can take a legitimate measure of pride, though as we shall see there is a debit side to the ledger.

It is a far cry from the small quantity of scholarly literature sent abroad by the Smithsonian Institution at the close of the nineteenth century to recent and current practice in this field. The number of books and periodicals given away for small sums or sold is large, but even so we have probably lagged behind. It may be said that this is not a business on which the American people embarked with signal pleasure. Indeed, they were probably pushed into it. The Nazis had given away inordinate quantities of *Mein Kampf* and of treatises written by such worthies as Alfred Rosenberg. The Russians outstripped them. After 1945 one could purchase in East or West Germany two leather-bound volumes of Lenin's works for the equivalent of fifty cents. Perhaps the most notable effort made by the United States in this area was to subsidize the publication, in a great variety of languages, of books considered to be of special value as propaganda. Sometimes these have been widely distributed. The committees of publishers which have advised the government on the matter have rendered excellent service. The whole effort has been under constant scrutiny.

### The exchange of persons

No doubt the area of the exchange of persons, in which the old Division of Cultural Relations had gingerly set foot, was the one most affected by postwar occupation requirements. The point is of interest because subsequent re-thinking has to a notable extent been occasioned by the experience gained. In 1945 the exchange program was considerably enlarged in order to bring about hoped for inoculations against totalitarian viruses. On the whole, it operated according to its own law of mutuality. Selected Americans were sent to Germany and Japan to meet with groups varied in character in order to convey to them a sense of the values which we strongly believed were characteristic of our society. On the other hand, people invited to visit the United States were usually selected from occupational groups thought most likely to influence public opinion in their countries.

This activity was certainly not without value, and it is doubtless regrettable that no reliable diagnosis of its achievements can be made at this late hour. Some things can very probably be accomplished through carefully shepherded excursions of this kind, even as there is something say for the Intourist methodology. Upon occasion more notable results have been obtained through quite modest confrontations arranged under private auspices. For example, the international conferences sponsored by Moral Rearmament at Caux, Switzerland, after 1945 ought not to have been successful if a variety of American opinions, ranging all the way from those of ribald skeptics to those entertained by Catholic and Protestant clergymen were to be credited. But the strange fact is that they *were*. Franco-German rapprochement owes to Caux a debt which must be inscribed on the pages of West European history.

### Comparative education

The General Advisory Committee had earlier recognized the importance of schools in the cultural program, so it was almost self-evident that in the post-war period the Japanese and German educator would figure prominently among the "exchangees." In the background were academic policies sponsored in the occupied countries on which we shall comment here only to point out that they were transitional between older forms of assistance given to American schools abroad and those which were advocated once the fury of the war had abated. The experience was instructive because it made evident that however impressive our educational achievements may be, it does not follow that our pedagogical practice will automatically impress everyone.

### THE COLD WAR AND ITS METHODOLOGY

The cold war soon called for its own methodology and orientation; and perhaps one may say that we of the United States were effective whenever we derived adequate benefit from the occupational experience. To begin with, the cold war immensely broadened the scope of our cultural activity. Then it gave this a radically different character. The Soviet Union was beyond any doubt determined to establish the dominion of communism over the world; and though it was at first difficult for many to believe that this was the case, the grim evidence became more and more overwhelming. One of communism's most thoroughly tested methods was forming elites, usually comprised of unhappy and unemployed intellectuals in disaffected areas, so that through them propaganda carefully tailor-made for the purpose could be widely disseminated. The most effective contention of that propaganda no doubt was that the Russian system was technically the most efficient and at the same time most ardently dedicated to peace. Since there was nothing in the Russian dictator's rule book which imposed an allegiance to truth, it was clear that the only way of dealing with him was to establish the fact that he was wrong and no doubt dangerously so.

### Cold War tasks of the United States

Therewith for its own salvation the United States was confronted with three tasks not at all easy to reconcile. The first was to try to persuade other peoples, among them the former German and Japanese enemies, that safety lay in a common military defensive system to which they must be expected to contribute. This has certainly never been easy. The second was counteracting Russian propaganda on both counts—that is, demonstrating the deep commitment of the American people to peace, and also conveying to needy peoples that this country was in possession of unparalleled technological ability which it stood ready to place, in so far as humanly possible, at the disposal of the peoples needing assistance. The third task was to familiarize other nations with the values for which American democracy stood, even while professing readiness to cherish differing cultural heritages in turn. For all these reasons the cold war greatly altered, in some respects revolutionized, the international outlook of the American people and therewith also its cultural relations program.

Certain activities, though they sometimes antedated the cold war, played a notable role in its waging. The International Cooperation Agency (The name has subsequently been altered although the structure of the operation remains pretty much the same. It is now the Agency for International Development.) carried out the worldwide commitments of the United States for technical and other forms of assistance. It proved to be the most diversified of governmental agencies, so difficult to survey or evaluate that it would require a staff of research workers to do so with any prospect of success. While many Americans are persuaded, for reasons which baffle analysis, that the Foreign Service Officer is usually a depraved character of minimal intelligence and loyalty to his country, the ICA official merited a special nomenclature providing for all degrees of ugliness. Of him or her it may, however, be said in general that an attempt was made to work to the best of human ability at a job which probably would have had critics speedily out of breath.

Sometimes as in West Berlin through ICA we made quite spectacular contributions to the progress of cultural relations. There a new library, right up against the Iron Curtain, and a complex of student residences built primarily to house young people from the Russian Zone who were bent on continuing their education at the Free University, testify to the occasional munificence and imaginativeness of the program. But most of the time the ICA man was dealing in Worthington pumps, agricultural know-how, and technical skill. Education in the development of technology at all levels has as a matter of fact been ICA's primary concern. Older exponents of a cultural relations policy would probably not have agreed that teaching relatively primitive communities such things as the organization of a street cleaning process was a vital part of what they had in mind. But in the world of the cold war, such jobs must precede what can later on be accomplished through the exchange of ideas.

This last-named form of exchange—the business of explaining what in terms of social and political doctrine the United States believes in and practices, why democratic institutions give a better account of themselves than do others, and how an open society can be be created—proves to be very difficult, indeed. If it is to be fruitful, at least two conditions would appear to be indispensable. First, the exchange of cultural values in this sense requires a special endowment of imagination and insight, *on both sides*. We Americans have tended of late to be far too critical of our spokesmen. When one is dealing with groups of foreign intellectuals who have no other deep-rooted desire than to acquire power and who will tailor any kind of ideology which seems likely to serve their purpose, no American, however intelligent, amiable and persuasive, is going to have much success. The second condition is that the teaching of cultural values in terms of the polity must be adapted to social and economic development. The statement is big with meaning, which can only be illustrated here. The two great social facts of our time are the growth of populations in the newly emerging countries and the rush of the surplus from rural areas to cities which cannot absorb them. These are formidable obstacles to the teaching of democratic values.

It must seem that one can only hope for progress in this realm through the multiple action of associations which combine disinterestedness with action. This conclusion appears to have underlain the interesting idea launched by President Eisenhower through the People to People program. He surmised that many undertakings in the area of cultural relations would thrive better if they were sponsored by private citizens rather than by government. A good deal of experience supports this view, and the President could effectively allude to it. American citizens had on their own initiative done such things as sending American books and periodicals to libraries abroad; mailing CARE parcels containing literature and school equipment; arranging for the adoption of cities and towns abroad by their counterparts in this country; subsidizing American studies programs in foreign universities; and making provision for fostering relationships between labor groups in this country and those overseas. Would it not be wise to coordinate, expand and support these efforts? The idea was only partially realized because adequate financing could not be obtained. But it was good none the less.

The President continued to be interested in what private groups were doing and in how their efforts could be more effectively coordinated with those of the federal government. A special post of Special Assistant to the Secretary of State was created (December, 1958) one of whose major tasks it was to explore the private sector so as to bring about a meeting of minds among those interested in international cultural activities. In the end, this not only provided a panoramic view of the almost innumerable commitments of private Americans abroad, but paved the way for more effective cooperation between them and the government. The scope of citizen activity in all the countries of the world to which Americans have access is breathtaking. It extends all the way from missionary endeavor by a variety of churches to the modest but fruitful work done by Letters Abroad to encourage correspondence between young people. Then there are any number of organizations diverse in character which have their special missions. And finally there are the great foundations. The fame of some of them is world-wide. Primitive people who go to bed not quite certain where the United States is have the name of the Rockefeller Foundation on their lips. It has helped to remove the scourge of disease, has supported charitable establishments, and has made two blades of grass grow where none did previously. Of late, The Ford Foundation has taken its honored place beside its older sister institution. Other foundations, the Kellogg Foundation and the Carnegie Foundation among them, have earned esteem both abroad and at home.

At this point it should be noted that the United States has learned to its sorrow that methods appropriate in one stage of the development of the Cold War are ineffectual or indeed deleterious in another. Thus after 1948 assistance was provided through an organization established by the Central Intelligence Agency for the training and participation of young citizens in international youth conferences. At that time the Soviet Union subsidized representatives of its own youth as well as of those considered friendly to it in other countries. Its objective was to take over organizations of young people such as the International Union of Students. As of that date this effort on the part of the Central Intelligence Agency was fully warranted. To argue otherwise is to manifest amnesia concerning aspects of the Cold War which were very real at the time. But continuing to provide support for the effort long after any visible need for it existed was to identify the cultural policy of the United States with purely counter-intelligence activities.

This process of identification reached a kind of climax with the Camelot affair, which created a furor during the summer of 1965. It concerned a project jointly sponsored by the American University of Washington, D.C., and the University of Chile, with financial support from the U. S. Army. The purpose was to study the ability of communist leaders to foment civil conflict and establish left-wing dictatorship in Latin American countries. Neither the Chilean Government nor the U.S. Ambassador had been informed. An attack in the Chilean congress on the project led to an investigation into "all activities which endanger our national sovereignty;" and at virtually the same time President Johnson instructed the Department of State to scrutinize all study projects being conducted by social scientists in Latin America with the help of funds allocated by our government. Perhaps nothing has set us back further. While on the one hand governmental action was designed to allay the fears of Latin American States, on the other hand it led to quite arbitrary decisions to curtail studies, however innocuous, already in progress.

In so far as libraries, surely one of the most commendable forms of between-nations intellectual cooperation, are concerned, Assistant Secretary for Cultural Affairs Charles Frankel has clearly shown that the identification of our libraries in some parts of the world with propaganda and intelligence activites is one reason for the attacks on them in Indonesia, Egypt and elsewhere. Those interested may be referred to his book, *The Neglected Aspect of Foreign Affairs*. In short, the instruments we use in the conduct of cultural affairs need to be adapted intelligently to the situation in which we at various times find ourselves.

The foundations, too, are human and have not always succeeded. It may also be that their targets, which they sought to reach through the application of science and technology to problems of human welfare, did not reckon sufficiently with humanistic culture. However that may be, the leadership and assistance they have provided in the areas of agriculture, medicine and the development of sciences has been of such inestimable value to the general cultural relations policy of the United States as a whole that one does not see how the progress made could have been effected without them. The foundations themselves do attempt to explain and in a sense advertise what they have accomplished. But it would be generally helpful if there could be made from "outside" a realistic and objective evaluation of their work.

CREATION OF INTERNATIONAL ORGANIZATIONS

Meanwhile there had taken place the creation and development of international organizations subsidiary to the United Nations. I have characterized some of them in an article for the *Saturday Review*, and shall borrow a few sentences from that:

> Concerned with the welfare of youth, with education, with the free exchange of dependable information, with the world's food supply and the conquest of disease, they now play a part in the affairs of men incalculably more significant than anyone could have foreseen ten years ago. . . . Nearly all of them engage in education. ILO fosters vocational training, UNICEF is concerned with the teaching of nutrition, WHO prepares leaders in Health Education. But by far the greatest share of the burden is carried by UNESCO, at all levels from elementary and adult education to the secondary school and the university.

Little in our national experience had prepared us for such joint action with other countries. Since the United States abstained from joining the League of Nations our relations with the International Institute of Intellectual Cooperation, set up under the League auspices, were informal. This was an organization which served the elite. But in 1945 we were called upon to assist in the creation of several bodies which would require of us support for and cooperation with international cultural endeavor.

*UNESCO*

Since UNESCO is from the point of view of cultural relations the most important of these organizations apart from the United Nations itself, it deserves attention. That some kind of international educational agency should be established was strongly urged by many even before the Second World War was ended. Men and women in allied governments responsible for planning the restoration of education in their countries once the war was over naturally thought of an international agency as a source of financial assistance and moral support. Various private groups, on the other hand, desired a consortium of peoples for the purpose of employing the educational resources of all to mitigate the hatreds which then seemed indispensable preludes to war. Moreover, there were scholars, notably natural scientists, who urged joint planning for the efficient exchange of information. The cause—viewed in any light—was certainly worthy.

The Charter of the United Nations was vague as to what the educational agency was to be. But during December of 1945 the matter was threshed out in London at a conference to which the United States sent a strong delegation. The United Nations Educational, Scientific and Cultural Organization (UNESCO) was created and given a constitution which reflected the mood and interests of the time, though it also determined with reasonable clarity what the powers of the organization were to be and what limitations were to be placed thereon. The overall objective was to foster peace by bringing about international understanding through education and cultural cooperation. But it was powerless to intervene in the affairs of any member state and could indeed function within any such state only upon explicit and specific request. This mandate was sometimes misunderstood or indeed deliberately misinterpreted.

## Implications of UNESCO

Supporting UNESCO meant that the United States was pledged henceforth to enter into a cooperative relationship with other peoples in order to bring about the fostering of education, science, and culture in the spirit of the United Nations. Initially, however, there was a disposition to believe that the government should be directly involved as little as possible, and that those who represented it should be men of eminence in their specialties who would be given a relatively free hand. This concept is reflected above all in the manner in which the United States National Commission for UNESCO was formed. The Commission was established by law as a group of one hundred, only a few of whom were to be nominated by the Department of State, while the great majority were to be designated by private organizations serving the multiform concerns of education in the broadest sense. It was believed that in this manner the triumph of the "grass roots" over bureaucracy would be assured.

But it soon became apparent that this early pattern was somewhat unrealistic. There were several reasons why this proved to be the case. First, more and more countries, with

Great Britain in the lead, turned the responsibility for UNESCO over to their Ministries of Education, thus following the lead given by the Allied Council of Ministers of Education during the war. Second, there was a natural though perhaps at first unanticipated tendency on the part of smaller nations to look upon UNESCO as an agency which could help them solve their educational problems through grants-in-aid. These grants might be outright gifts of money or of the services of specialists. The pressure on the wealthier countries could not be kept within reasonable bounds unless governments exercised appropriate diplomatic leadership. Finally, the entry of the Soviet Union and her satellites into UNESCO, some nine years after its establishment, meant the transfer to this forum of the cold war debate which was so marked a characteristic of the United Nations itself. The Department of State was necessarily compelled to promote its policies through normal diplomatic means.

These difficulties became more obvious as the significance of UNESCO increased. The newer nations began to take stock of their educational needs; and whether the region was Asia, the Near East, Latin America or Africa, the outline of what there was to do resembled a contour map of mountains more formidable than the Himalayas, to be scaled somehow. Soon, the United Nations, too, was deeply involved in this startling new adventure of the human mind. Planning became the primary necessity. UNESCO was now not so much a symbol of hope that the world as a whole would see the task as its own, as it was a working partner. More and more money was funneled into it from a variety of sources tapped by the United Nations— Technical Assistance, the Special Fund, the International Development Association, the Inter-American Development Bank. Such an enterprise, farflung in every sense, had to rely more and more on the good will and assistance of the United States, which in turn was of necessity impelled to meet the challenge.

*Future relations with UNESCO and the U.N.*

There can be little doubt, therefore, that relationships with UNESCO, as of the present and in the future, must play a more important part in the thinking and planning of the Department of State. The responsibilities of the organiz-ation will increase; the hopes entertained throughout the world for educational advancement must be supported, and the problems of organization and personnel will require closer attention. Even if the critics of UNESCO were cor-rect, the steps taken in 1945 and 1946, when the first Gen-eral Conference convened in Paris, could not now be re-traced. The organization is so badly needed and so popular in many parts of the world that we cannot any longer imagine what international cultural activity would be like if UNESCO did not exist. One must note also that just as the Department of State has utilized private groups to administer programs, so has UNESCO, and it will doubt-less continue to do so, perhaps even more than in the past. The point is of some importance in connection with our own planning.

Meanwhile the cultural relations function of the U.N. it-self has become highly important as its "service activities" have increased. Its peace-keeping endeavors are at their lowest ebb; and some by no means obstreperous critics feel that these activities will have little significance for some time to come. But who can question the beneficence of the UN in other important areas? For one thing it has had a part of great importance to play in bringing about a marked reduction in the radiation after-effects of nuclear explo-sions; and through its influence in effecting the policy gov-erning the peaceful uses of nuclear energy it has rendered priceless service in the prevention of the transformation of industrial plants into armories serving the direct form of war. Moreover, leadership provided by it in setting up universally respected international conferences on the prob-lems of economic and social development has made it, from the point of view of the United States, quite indispensable.

## THE EXPERIENCE GAINED

Before proceeding to consider what the policy of the United States might be during the years which lie ahead, however tentatively we may define those years, we shall summarize the principal decisions reached in the past con-cerning cultural policy. They are:

1. That the exchange of persons, at all levels of the na-tion's activity, is a major concern of cultural policy, for the

following reasons: it brings about a flow in two directions of personalized information, experience and understanding; it affords the people of the United States an opportunity to acquaint others with the character of our social and cultural institutions; it broadens above all the outlook of teachers; and it emphasizes the concept of freedom in the context of learning.

2. That the concept of freedom is of vital importance, because the function of propaganda, which is formalized and directed learning about a country or a point of view, is of limited value except in times of conflict.

3. That books, periodicals and documentation in forms associated with the term "visual aids" (including radio and television broadcasts) are important resources of cultural policy, especially when distributed in ways which themselves illustrate the character of American life—one such way being the open shelf library.

4. That cultural affairs officers represent the United States effectively and meaningfully when they are truly cultivated persons, above all in the sense that they have expert acquaintance with the countries in which they serve.

5. That the government can in many instances achieve more fruitful results in this field if, even in the area of assistance programs, it entrusts the responsibility for putting programs into operation to private organizations and agencies, since these are less likely to suggest propaganda aims.

6. That the efforts of private persons and groups in the area of cultural exchange should be encouraged by the government; with the understanding that, when possible, they are to be properly coordinated, without dictation, with what the government itself is undertaking.

7. That international cultural organizations, notably UNESCO, should be vigorously supported because they can in some instances obtain results which no government acting in isolation can expect to obtain, because they are invaluable centers of consultation, inquiry and documentation, and also because, realistically considered, they represent a frugal investment from the point of view of the United States.

All these decisions have now been amply tested and their value has been proved. It is of course true that there is much room for improvement in virtually all respects. But looking back over a period of barely twenty years, we may say that the United States has made great strides forward in developing a cultural relations policy and program. Admittedly it would probably never have developed had not armed conflict and cold warfare made their impact on the national thinking. Henceforth a new kind of worldwide revolution will unquestionably spur us on to even greater effort. The necessity in which whole continents now find themselves to pass quickly from quite primitive conditions to forms of social living in which urbanization and industrialization will play important roles brings education to the fore as the indispensable prelude to world commerce and understanding. This fact alone will give cultural relations a new dimension.

There are other facts as well. One is the possibility of failure. If efforts to bring about so startling a change in the affairs of new nations should bog down, these will no longer even have the support of the primitive, oral cultures which hitherto have given the lives of masses depth and significance, despite poverty and other ills. Nor in all probability could the deterioration be localized. It would engender conflict and upheaval which might well spread even as the plagues of yore. Clearly one way to prevent such a breakdown is continued, vigorous, and cooperative action by the United Nations.

### Political implications of cultural policy

It had become apparent by the time the Congo crisis signaled the end of colonialism in Africa and the emergence on the world stage of a continent of new nations that cultural relations could no longer be shunted off the mainstream of United States foreign policy. One of the principal issues in that crisis was whether the educational system established by the Belgians could be maintained and brought into closer harmony with the nature and aspirations of the independent state which would now enter history. As part of his effort to forestall Russian assumption of leadership in the Congo and a possible war, President Eisenhower sponsored a grant of support to the United Nations for educational and cultural action. This meant, of course, that this action was seen as a vital part of the policy of serving the best interests of the United States through diplomacy.

The administration of President Kennedy immediately took an important step forward by appointing an Assistant Secretary of State for Educational and Cultural Affairs. Consultation was taken with panels of experts to determine the character of what had been and could be done to make the efforts of the United States more effective. Reports of findings were made. More recently (February, 1962), the Assistant Secretary, acting under the authority of the new Fulbright-Hays Act, formed an advisory group, the United States Advisory Commission on International Educational and Cultural Affairs, which to all intents and purposes recreated the old General Advisory Committee to the Division of Cultural Relations, though to be sure the scope is broader and the means with which to act far greater. In the intervening period a number of other Advisory Commissions had been created, one of which had been the United States Advisory Commission on Educational Exchange which is now superseded.

In 1960 this Commission had invited Dr. Walter H. C. Laves to prepare a report. This is entitled *Toward a National Effort in International Educational and Cultural Affairs* (Department of State Publication 7238). This is warmly recommended to everyone who desires to study in greater depth the problems and opportunities now before the nation. Dr. Laves considers the "general foreign policy objectives" of United States cultural programs:

> Some should be designed primarily to advance knowledge and to strengthen the world community of education, science and culture.
>
> Some programs should be designed primarily to develop an understanding abroad of United States culture and institutions.
>
> Some programs should be designed primarily to develop among the American people understanding of other people and their cultures and institutions.
>
> Some should be designed primarily to make available specialized knowledge and skills to countries at different levels of development.
>
> Finally, some programs should be designed to strengthen the development of democratic societies and other institutions in other countries.

## A Theory of Cultural Relations

If this is accepted, as no doubt it should be, as an accurate statement of major objectives in the field of cultural relations, there will be a number of important questions to ask and to answer. Prior to dealing with some of them we may, however, consider with a measure of profit whether a theory of cultural relations can be devised, as distinguished from a pragmatic appraisal of the experience so far gained. Any effort to deal with such a theory must, however, be venturesome and tentative, because no probing study of the problems involved has been made. In the United States one can begin with the sound basic assumption that at the present stage of human history a developed national society tends for the sake of its own stability and welfare to take on an international dimension. We doubtless see this clearly in those areas of activity which are most easily measurable in terms of the national interest. Thus, it is devoutly to be wished that further agreements can be reached with the Soviet Union concerning the control of outer space and disarmament, at least insofar as nuclear weapons are involved. Seen in the light of such developments, extreme isolationist groups in the United States must seem retrogressive. The "international dimension" is inevitable.

### What is the "international dimension"?

The "international dimension" will of course in many respects not be the same for us as it is for other nations of the free world. We have at times succeeded in beating the United Nations into the kind of ploughshare we need because it could at least achieve a measure of effectiveness as a buffer between ourselves and the Russians. It has functioned at best with a creaking of gears and engines lined with carbon. That some friendly powers have not eyed the scene with exhilaration is understandable. Upon occasion, certainly with good reason, they have watched the process of majority building in the United Nations and its specialized agencies with doubts and misgivings.

We find ourselves in a comparable situation insofar as cultural relations are concerned, though great differences exist. What is the "international dimension" in cultural relations? The answer is, free trade in cultural goods. And what are these goods? They may, I think, be defined as those accretions of information, inquiry and creative artistic achievement which are the concerns of the modern university. Intellectually considered, they may conveniently be summarized as the accumulation of knowledge and method which the human mind has built up round those fundamental, reality-revealing intuitions which in their totality form the present outlook of mankind. Thus, in the natural sciences we have developed a great expanse of instrumentalities of investigation and technological achievement around the insights gained by men of genius from Euclid to Einstein, Planck, De Broglie and Heisenberg. In the study of society we have moved from Plato and the Mosaic injunctions to the behavioral sciences. Religion, philosophy, and the arts have added their own intuitions and have created round them vast literatures and important programs of action. With all these the modern university is concerned in terms both of knowledge and of inquiry.

But the university does not exist for its own sake alone. It is the source from which the lower schools draw sustenance and inspiration. Thus, the teaching of English literature in a good secondary school today is very different from what it was a generation or two ago, because university scholarship has altered both the approach to aesthetics and the contour of the historical situation in which every book must necessarily be written. We are all very much aware these days that mathematics and physics cannot be taught effectively unless the teacher comprehends in some measure at least the concepts which now underlie these sciences. To use still another illustration, the teaching of languages in our time has been radically changed by the application of the findings of linguistics.

Quite as memorable is the manner in which the university has modified and is modifying the methods of work and the employment of leisure time. It is not merely that mechanization has been a highly revolutionary influence, though it has been that to almost an incalculable extent, but also that in our society at least the working man has been freed from kinds of bondage and dependence which were normal a century ago. This is in part due to the development of social ethics and the social sciences. Even the mass media, which with us seem anti-intellectual or at least addicted to circuses, tend in curious ways and normal ones to reflect the progress of research. Thus, television has familiarized nearly everybody with the weather map, triumph of careful meteorological observation over many years. And, in a different vein, every listener to modern police reporting and detective fiction will be able to tell you that the defense attorney in Dostoievski's *Brothers Karamazov* was ignorant of modern techniques in the detection of criminals.

At the level of the university in the strict sense, the "international dimension" has long since been a routine matter. For example, in former days, when it was taken for granted that an understanding of classical languages and literatures was equivalent to a liberal education, the philologists of two centuries toiled to establish texts as nearly perfect as the most scrupulous study could manage. There was no country in Europe which did not furnish its quota of scholars for the task, and what one created became the property of all. The fact that every advanced student of the humanities was required to know several languages—normally Latin, French and German—also testifies to the fact that scholarship did not stop at national boundaries. For a considerable length of time, research in the natural sciences followed the same pattern. Kepler, Copernicus, Pascal and Newton spoke to their peers wherever in the world these were listening. It was only after the Industrial Revolution and the beginnings of modern warfare that the applications of scientific discovery to manufacturing and armament made secrecy on a large scale the rule.

Today the trend is once again strongly in the direction of exchange. In spite of the cold war, it has been possible for UNESCO, with the assistance of American and British scientists, to sponsor effective international research in geophysics, soil aridity and oceanography. The Russians have effectively cooperated with all these efforts. The tradition of the university has overcome other barriers as well. Exchanges in the fields of literature and economics have been resumed on a world-wide scale. Western-oriented countries have gone back since the close of the Second World War to traditional ways of making known the products of research. Indeed—exception having duly been made for the applications of science which are protected by patents or are kept under mantles of secrecy by governments—the sole problem existing at present is how to assimilate what is being offered. The sum-total of facts collected is enormous.

### The factors of ignorance and prejudice

But as soon as one comes down from this high perch (It may be noted that members of university faculties are also human, upon occasion distressingly human.) there is a different story to tell. We must reckon with the factors of ignorance and prejudice. Let us look at ignorance first. Restrictions on the free flow of information continue to erect mighty barriers between peoples. They are first of all artificially created by governments or private groups. But poverty also plays a part, inhibiting the gathering and dissemination of both news and comment. Many believe that the situation as a whole has deteriorated rather than improved since the close of the Second World War. But there are two other persistent kinds of ignorance. The first is lack of education, which in its worst form may be illiteracy, though in view of what a great many people read one is sometimes inclined to doubt it. The second is specialization, which may so absorb a man's time and attention that his view of the world tends to become one-sided or indeed myopic.

When one bears these handicaps in mind, it is not easy to be confident that for the great majority of the world's peoples the "international dimension" in terms of cultural relations will soon prove very significant. Yet there are relationships even where we should not expect to find them. For instance, people round the world dearly love to travel, even if they can do so only vicariously by talking with someone who has come from a far country. The magic carpet of the *Arabian Nights* is one of the oldest and best distributed resources of the human imagination. People are attracted by the exotic, provided it remains within what they would consider reasonable bounds. And of course nearly everyone has a bundle of images of certain foreign places, based on sailors' yarns, movies, television and something or other handed down in the family. Paris is a city of sin, Essen is a place where Germans work hard and therefore succeed, Rome is where the Pope lives, and Cairo is full of belly dancers.

The barriers of prejudice are erected close to the images. It is unnecessary to discuss them in detail, or indeed to attempt to isolate the factor of prejudice in the area of cultural relations. But knowledge that it is a world-wide reality, shifting with the times, so that in any society a prejudice may speedily give way to its opposite, greatly affects one's views as to the beneficence of mutual exchange of cultural goods as opposed to propaganda. Prejudice entertained against the United States, for example, is usually rooted in things its citizens have done or are supposed to have done. Tourists have been noisy and obstreperous. Soldiers have misbehaved. And so on. Will all be well if one substitutes people who are models of decorum and wisdom—if one, for example, multiplies Peace Corps contingents? Or will it be desirable to provide a full-dress campaign to advertise the virtues of the American people and thus create a different image?

These are some of the problems with which a working theory of cultural relations will perforce deal. There are others, some of them crucial, for example that of how to utilize the earlier years of education in order to develop a greater readiness to approach other cultures with an open mind. But, if the assumption that an "international dimension" is a plain fact can be considered correct, certain things may be predicted from the American point of view concerning the whole area of life which the university indirectly influences but does not control. First, there will be a certain motivation among peoples abroad to know about the United States, and, conversely, a comparable motivation here to learn more about other countries. Second, having defined the motivation, one can plan more or less realistically to satisfy it. Third, the plan must provide for unity of purpose while projecting the use of highly diversified means.

To attempt a definition of the motivation in question is far from easy. For my part I would say the basic urges are primarily utilitarian but by no means exclusively so. Everyone admires certain kinds of American technological achievement. But unfortunately few other nations consider that our experience in the conduct of government is of use to them. They do not know how to practice our form of parliamentary democracy, and it is very doubtful that they will try hard to do so. An Egyptian will judge Nasser by how well he succeeds in benefiting the rank and file, and not by now he does it, provided he does not resort to wholesale massacre or suppress religion. But there are other urges, too, and some of them are quite different in character.

For example, the fact that the United States has been represented abroad by great philanthropic organizations, notably the Ford and Rockefeller Foundations, has identified this country with unselfish concern for general human welfare. They have carried on a secular program, supplementing in notable ways the activities of missionary groups, which for a long time carried the burden of education in many areas of the world. Efforts as diverse as the struggle to remove the scourges of yellow fever and malaria, the painstaking work to preserve the monuments of Pharaonic culture in Egypt, and the patient development of improved agricultural methods—all carried on without a thought of personal advantage to the donors—have left memories of service and good will which cannot, one thinks, be eradicated. They have formed an image of the American people which is invaluable for us.

### National interests and cultural relations

But if one looks at these things more closely, it will become evident that the interests of a culture or a people are always involved. National feeling in Africa is necessarily (though not always realistically) anti-colonial, both because there could have been no nationhood while a colony existed, and because the colonial idea was based on the assumption that the people governed were inferior. And yet it does not follow that the erstwhile colonial relationship, say with Great Britain, will be abrogated in favor of an all-out espousal of American ways or ideas. The new peoples have first of all become used to dealing with the British, to accepting their patterns of education and of speech, and to profiting by often genuinely effective efforts made by the British both to assist the people under colonial rule and to continue that assistance after independence had been gained. The United States is, of course, acclaimed as a source from which economic and technical assistance on a grand scale can be expected. On the other hand, there exist in the United States forms of race feeling which for a long time have not flourished under British rule.

The "international dimension" of the United States is therefore in this instance a two-sided reality. On the one hand, it is not a nation with a colonial past, despite "dollar diplomacy" and temporary imperialist adventures. On the other hand, there is projected from it into the post-colonial world a theory and practice of race relations which summon to mind some of the worst aspects of colonialism. In the long run, attrition may well take its natural course. That is, memories of the colonial past will recede, as they have with us; and the pattern of race relations in the United States will no doubt improve. But at the present time the handicap exists and it is no doubt a serious one.

It would therefore seem that in theory the best way to proceed in some post-colonial countries in terms of cultural relations at the extra-university level would be to accept the reality which the British, the French or others have created and to cooperate with it to the fullest extent possible while taking advantage of every opportunity within reason to foster mutually beneficial exchanges of our own. This would would mean less concentration on the anti-communist program and more on inter-Western cooperation. Such activities as Operation Crossroads Africa are no doubt potentially very effective. Nevertheless, in theory, they would be still more productive of desirable results, if it were possible to coordinate them with what European nations are doing. Unquestionably our "international dimension" as a whole is clouded by a far too restricted appreciation of the cultural strength of Western Europe.

A comparable situation exists in Latin America. Perhaps the developments in Cuba may serve as an example. It seemed evident that economic assistance could come from us alone, and this actually was the case until the espousal of Castro by the Soviet Union. But Cuba had continued, despite the vicissitudes of history, to be in many ways an outpost of Spanish culture. The Spanish revolutionary tradition influenced the outlook of those who were opposed to the established dictatorship. On the other hand the clergy were predominantly Spanish in origin, and no real effort was made to recruit a native clergy. Religion was associated with middle-class prejudices (The fact that Castro was an illegitimate child was emphasized during his early years.) and had no conceptual formulation insofar as the common people were concerned. Accordingly the too easy assumption by the United States that economic assistance could and would continue to create a desired favorable relationship was proved startlingly mistaken. More serious concern for cultural realities and values, as well as greater expert insight into the character of Spanish thought, might well have found us better prepared to judge the revolutionary situation in Cuba and deal with it effectively. For various reasons scholarship and education in the United States have had during recent years only a tenuous relationship with Spanish culture.

In Latin America as a whole, our economic and strategic interests have often been opposed to those of the native populations. As a result, in the area of cultural relations, "freedom" from their point of view has generally been something radically different from what it has been from ours. We have coveted a free hand in banning European influences we consider undesirable, in conducting business and investing capital, and in fostering spiritual and intellectual movements reflecting our own cultural pattern. But when the Latin American has conjured up the notion of freedom, he has thought in the first instance of a long history of military actions taken by his neighbor to the north. He has remembered the Mexican War, the Spanish-American War, the building of the Panama Canal, and the punitive expedition set in motion by President Wilson. The two concepts have clashed over a long period and have of course led to a measure of exploitation, real or fancied, and on the other hand to the confiscation of capital investments. Regardless of who has been right or wrong, older attitudes still underlie the otherwise very impressive structure of international cooperation which has more recently been erected.

Therefore when we speak of the free exchange of cultural goods, we must see to it that both Latin America and we understand the terms the same way. Otherwise the ship will sink before the cargo leaves port. Many young Latins come to the United States in quest of an education, and profit by it. Many more study English—indeed, English will very likely become the second language of Latin America. But actually the amount of cultural exchange and its quality leave very much to be desired. In one respect we try too hard, perhaps, and in another not hard enough. Anxiety to keep Latin America safe for ourselves and the free world is a highly laudable emotion. We should have begun to feel it sooner. Unquestionably, sending young Americans to Chile as members of the Peace Corps was an excellent idea, but, just as certainly, inviting a comparable group of young Latin Americans to come here would be equally commendable. The Latin American university has little to offer us in the natural and social sciences. But it does have much in the humanities and the arts.

### The free flow of cultural goods

One may state by way of summary: motivation in the area of cultural exchange derives from the conviction that the free flow of cultural goods will be to the advantage of the participating peoples and states, though it may not immediately affect other interests of a political or economic character. This conviction is supported by an almost universal belief that education is a blessing in which all the sons of men can share. Yet there are special things to say about it. While politics and economics are tested and served by action—in free states, both private and governmental action—and to a limited but still important sense by propaganda, the free flow of cultural goods will be most effective when it exists for its own sake. To be sure, it will be benefited and not hampered by what may be termed effective salesmanship. Common sense dictates, for example, that when exchange fellowships are made available, they should be given to the grantees with as few commitments as possible. The accepted reason should be that those who obtain them will have an opportunity to see and learn as much as possible of what they *wish* to see and learn. Nevertheless, the mere fact that the scholarships are offered is propagandistic in character and must be recognized as being so.

Since, as has been said, cultural values are, for the most part, the products of the university, conceived of now in the broadest possible sense, it is important to see what the university's objectives are. One may answer that ideally it is committed to the unhampered and fearless confrontation of man with reality, and that therefore it is the most powerful force which can be pitted against ignorance and prejudice. At all levels of education or human experience which it controls or influences, it desires the largest possible measure of conformity with its own spirit. But we must be realistic and add that in the present world situation the university can also unfortunately be an instrument or a slave. The communist university, whether in Russia or the satellite states, is in important areas of thought restricted to a program of indoctrination. It must teach the social sciences not as they are, but as the government of the Soviet Union desires them to be. Nor can the arts, philosophy or religion be discussed with an open mind. Consequently, we need to assume, when we as citizens of the United States undertake to promote or share in the free flow of cultural goods, that we must act in the spirit of the great, traditional university of the West, and that as a result propaganda for it, overt or implicit, is an essential component part of the action.

Propaganda, however, must never ignore the essential issue: what is needed and desired is freedom of inquiry and of choice. Accordingly, the stream must always move in two ways. Cultural relations can be effective only when minds *meet*. An American university in Cairo will prove worthwhile and beneficent if those who teach in it learn to know Egypt even while imparting specifically American kinds of knowledge. Operation Crossroads Africa will succeed only as those who comprise it acquire insight into the country they are serving.

If what has been said about motivation in the realm of cultural relations and about the complex situations in which it functions is accepted with at least a measure of assent, two things follow: first, the program as a whole must be designed to promote a free flow of cultural goods at three levels—that of the education of the trained elite, that of the formal teaching of the schools, and that of what is termed adult education; second, each single effort must be carefully planned and just as carefully put into practice. Concerning the first, it may be said that while it may not always be possible to work on all three levels, none can be neglected in theory. There is often a tendency to ignore one or the other on the basis of assumed principle. Thus our cultural programs, both public and private, tended during the period between the two World Wars to concentrate on the trained elite. Most of them were as a matter of fact the endeavors of the learned societies acting with some measure of government support. After 1945 there was a tendency to assume that only an effort to reach the grass roots was any longer realistic. Of course, there was a great deal to say in favor of both positions. Let us as a consequence accept both.

### The problem of coordination

One may then proceed to say that while a measure of coordination of what is done by government with what is achieved by private groups is desirable, and that accordingly while the efforts to that end made by the Department of State are to be commended, it is gravely to be doubted that government ought to attempt to set up any sort of plan with the expectation that private citizens or groups should be controlled by it. I am of course not speaking here of these when acting as agents for the government, nor can there be any question that coordination is upon occasion imperative. Good examples are the manner in which Hungarian students in exile were assimilated by our institutions of higher education, and the intervention of the Department of State to rescue African students from the near disaster in which many of them found themselves when private adventures in student exchange broke down. Normally, however, the free flow of cultural goods will be assisted if private initiative and indeed tradition are given free rein. Some confusion and some duplication of effort must be anticipated, but the plain fact of the matter is that no government agency has either the time or the omniscience which are needed to draw up an over-all blueprint for everyone to follow.

But obviously government should have a blueprint for its own activities, which ought to be projected as far into the future as possible. It should take into consideration all of the various instrumentalities of cultural exchange, and bring these into a desirable alignment. This is very difficult to do during times dominated by military concerns, and from these we have had virtually no respite since 1945. The United States has had to deal in succession with situations in Greece, Korea, the Dominican Republic, the Middle East, Vietnam and elsewhere. These interventions and their after-maths have diverse, often irreconcilable effects on cultural policy. On the one hand they tend to emphasize the worst consequences of American influence, including payment for low class entertainment and sexual indulgence. On the other hand they are usually accompanied by efforts to im-prove education and the social services in the countries in-volved. Every U.S. occupation force is from the point of view of the population affected both a burden and a boon.

In other respects more coordination than now exists seems eminently desirable, in spite of improvements ef-fected. The results of membership in the U.N. and its sub-sidiary organization are still computed separately from those gained from other efforts in the area of cultural policy. Much of this failure is of course due to the ambivalence of public opinion. The U.N. has numerous active friends, but is still widely associated with a popular feeling that it threatens the independence and the stability of the United States. Just why we should want to go it alone in such fields as educational planning or educational and social develop-ment is a question difficult to answer. But at present some groups of citizens and their representatives seem to prefer isolation.

Granted the overall unity of effort suggested, it will soon become apparent that each project needs to be endowed at all times with its own individuality. If a program is to suc-ceed in France, it will have to be designed for France. And yet one cannot any longer think of that country without bearing in mind that it is now placed, more than ever be-fore, in a European context. In like manner, if something really effective is to happen in Africa, it must be planned for some region or state in particular, while the continental dimensions of the total African effort are borne in mind. This is extremely difficult to do. There are doubtless not nearly enough people available to get this and other jobs done. And so it may be asked whether, at this stage in the planning, it might not be wise to use the services of experts from abroad just as we have employed them in atomic and rocket research.

### Summary

At any rate, this is a tentative theory of cultural relations which can no doubt be greatly improved. It may be restated briefly:

In our time, every highly developed country has taken on an "international dimension" which means interaction with other countries and regions.

The "international dimension" in cultural relations is the free flow of cultural goods. These are essentially the concern of the modern university, either directly or through the lower schools and the instrumentalities of mass education and public opinion.

The obstacles to the free flow of cultural goods are primarily: artificial curbs of cultural traffic, ignorance and prejudice. These are formidable obstacles, but there exists a powerful motivation to surmount them.

This motivation is the product of a conviction that a free flow of cultural goods, to and fro, will serve the individual nation's interests, sometimes directly but also upon occasion indirectly.

These interests will be best served if as far as possible the spirit of the university, which is that of the unhampered and fearless confrontation of man and reality, is conserved. But in view of the divided world it cannot always be conserved.

So much being taken for granted, it follows that the cultural relations program of the United States must have a unity of objective but a marked diversity and flexibility of approach.

The unity should be sought not through an impossible endeavor to bring public and private efforts into some kind of artificially created bundle but by cross-reference between the great variety of government activities, correlated as fully as possible with private effort.

By diversity is meant the realistic, well-informed adaptation of each activity to the target with which it is concerned.

## Two General Problems

We shall, in the light of what has been said, consider very briefly two general problems which government must always face when it acts in the dimension of cultural relations. The first is the problem of adaptation of personnel policies; the second is the problem of exchanges.

### *Adaptation of personnel policies*

It is fairly obvious that when we think of cultural relations we must bear in mind both our country's involvement on its own initiative, whether voluntarily taken or enforced by reason of the international situation, and its association with other countries already at work in a given area. With some of these countries we might well seek to cooperate, while opposition to others will prove unavoidable. In other words, there are practically no parts of the world in which we can find and appropriate virgin territory. Second, it should be apparent that cultural relations activity in a country with an old and rich literary culture will have to assume a character quite different from that of a program to be carried out in a country which is still close to an oral tradition, or has perhaps wholly lost a sense of tradition. In both instances a considerable measure of tact is required; and tact—apart from being a mysterious something one either has or hasn't—may be defined as adequate orientation for the task involved.

Manifestly not everyone who represents the United States on a cultural mission will have the experience or the receptivity which would ideally be required. Yet it is very important that some should. One cannot expect the average lecturer, exchange student, technician or even Fulbright scholar to be more than his nation has equipped him to be. But our country needs to provide, in intimate association with them, at least one or two persons who serve as symbols because they are accepted as equals and friends by the cultural leaders of the countries to which they are sent. This does not mean that they are to associate only with the elite. On the contrary, in some countries a professor who speaks the language may make his greatest impact on the common people generally. Finding such men and using them is a difficult task, particularly since the Foreign Service is not organized to recruit them or to use their services over more than brief periods of time. Cultural relations from the career point of view are far from being competitive at present either in interest or importance with the conduct of diplomacy serving the major political or economic interests of our country's advancement.

Another major difficulty is the mobility of the Foreign Service, and still another the mantle of security every officer must constantly wear. No sooner has a man prepared himself well for a cultural mission and thoroughly familiarized himself with the life of a country than he is whisked off the premises and sent to a wholly different part of the world. The mantle of security which must be worn if the diplomatic business is to succeed is for its part a grave handicap because if a Foreign Service officer consorts too freely with aliens he may inadvertently find himself in water no longer lukewarm.

No doubt the general provisions governing the Foreign Service cannot be changed in any notable way. But it might be interesting to consider whether the category of Cultural Attachés could not be so established that it would depend upon its own recruitment procedures and also have a promotion and advancement schedule of its own. This last might be comparable to what prevails in academic life. Were this done, the Department might also find it possible to deviate from the normal rules of rotation and so allow a good officer to remain in the country with which he is familiar for a longer period. If all this were once agreed upon, it should prove easier to enlist the kind of men and women needed for the task, and map out careers for them which would be equal in terms of rewards of several kinds —intellectual as well as monetary—to what they could have earned in the American college or university. A cultural relations program will be no better than are those appointed to carry it out. Changes in method or increases in the amount of materials made available will not in the long run achieve the objectives sought unless the people to whom the mechanism is entrusted are genuinely first-rate. This truth remains important also when there is question of those who are to do the everyday chores associated with various kinds of cultural or assistance programs. Most of them will be on short-term assignments, and what matters, therefore, is their ability to carry out these while not doing harm. The number of those so employed is growing steadily, which almost automatically suggests that the quality cannot be uniformly high.

The whole problem and the data on the basis of which it can profitably be considered have been outlined in a number of publications, two of which will be singled out here: *Americans at Work Abroad* and *The Overseas Americans*, by Harlan Cleveland and others. The points of view expressed in these volumes cannot be brought into focus here, but the reader will encounter verities which probably had to be accepted during the earlier stages of the foreign aid or mutual assistance programs, and which should slowly but surely be restudied. A large number of American citizens are now sent abroad either by the United States government or by private organizations and foundations. Some of these have been or are obviously misfits. This is not at all surprising, nor is it peculiarly American. Not everybody who is employed by a college as an instructor survives the period of initiation. Nor, strange as it may seem to perusers of some currently popular literature, is every Russian who goes to a foreign area an exemplar of tact, ability, morality and plain common sense.

But, as the authors of a valuable survey of the situation and of the pertinent literature, Frank N. and Helen G. Trager, ("Exporting and Training Experts," in the *Review of Politics*) have indicated, some steps can no doubt be taken to bring about improvement. One is in recruiting. In all probability, the government has tended to overrate the factor of youth and to discount maturity. There is, of course, not a little to be said in favor of the policy so far in force. First, the young can *probably* cope more effectively with the climatic and other hardships encountered on some missions. On the basis of personal experience, I rather doubt this; and I suspect that a careful review of missionary history would support the legitimacy of the question mark. Second, it is very likely true that on the whole men and women past forty-five are so firmly rooted in what they are doing that it is often difficult, indeed, to pry them loose for foreign service. Yet it would seem that there are sources of supply which could be tapped, particularly for personnel who are to remain on a mission for some time.

Another change called for is in the process of orientation. At the present time, Washington normally supplies some weeks of instruction, which is beyond all doubt desirable but which must in the very nature of things be inadequate. It follows, therefore, that some additional orientation in the country of assignment ought to be provided. It might well be worth considering whether in areas where programs of some size and duration are contemplated, a center of orientation should not be set up wherein veterans from the United States and carefully selected native educators or officials would join forces to prepare during an additional period recruits for effective work.

### The exchange of persons

The important and central question of the exchange of persons came of age insofar as the government is concerned with legislative acts which retain in this area of activity a significance comparable to that of the land grant legislation in the history of our educational system. The Fulbright Amendment, which was the expression of an imaginative approach to the problem of restoring cultural ties that had been broken off as a result of the Second World War, was followed by the Smith-Mundt Act and, more recently, by the Fulbright-Hays Act, which greatly enlarges the scope of cultural relations, though not providing funds with which to do so. These are impressive illustrations of how the importance of cultural exchanges has been understood by the Congress.*

There are several ways in which the problem involved can be formulated, and we cannot review all of them. It

---

* The Fulbright Act of 1946 provided for the use of foreign currency balances accruing abroad for mutual cultural exchanges. The Smith-Mundt Act of 1948 provided limited dollar support particularly for foreign scholars coming to the United States, the total amount available being determined annually by the Congress. The Agricultural Trade and Development and Assistance Act of 1954 earmarked funds accruing abroad from the sale of surplus agricultural commodities abroad for exchange purposes. The Fulbright-Hays Act of 1961 very considerably broadened the exchange program, but no provision was made in this Act for funds with which to implement it.

must suffice to indicate that the basic reason why anybody wishes to go to another country to study is that he can, or at least thinks he can, learn something he would not learn if he stayed at home. He may be mistaken, or what he has in mind may be of trivial value, but the target is of sufficient interest to induce him to take the trouble. In large part, *directed* cultural exchange is a matter of identifying things which ought to be learned about, and then finding people one thinks can and will learn them. That, for example, is pretty much what happens when The Ford Foundation establishes a program of fellowships for foreign study.

In view of the relative ratios of development, between, say, technology in the United States and scientific illiteracy in Liberia, directed research in our time must often be heavily weighted. That is, we set out to learn, broadly speaking, *about* some peoples, and they learn *from* us. Neither process is easy. The first may be qualitatively more difficult, but the second is from the quantitative point of view vastly more exacting. It is said, for example (though one may not wish to vouch for the accuracy of the computation), that ninety per cent of all scientists who ever lived are alive now. But why are they alive now? Because a very great deal of time, money and talent have been expended on building up institutions in which scientists could be trained and given opportunity to do research. Obviously by comparison, sub-tropical Africa, where only a single university owns a nuclear reactor, has to learn from us, or from other countries comparably experienced and staffed, if it hopes to add significantly to the number of scientists. And this again will cost a great deal of time, money and talent.

Learning about a country is hardly a science but an art. Learning from a country is hardly an art but a science. To expound this difference would require a volume, were it to be attempted with the requisite thoroughness. We shall merely note that there are, in the main, two ways of learning to know a country. The first is through making a careful study of some aspects of its history, customs, physical characteristics and institutions. The second way is to study the culture—or perhaps one should borrow a term from psychologists and say the *Gestalt*—of a country so thoroughly and imaginatively that one comes to see it from the inside. One may then still be mistaken in estimating the course it will take historically, by reason of irrational and other factors—but one's errors will be those of the people one has come to know and not those of an outsider.

The second consideration, namely that some countries seek to learn from us, was discussed by the then Assistant Secretary of State for Educational and Cultural Affairs, Philip H. Coombs in a significant and intelligent address entitled, "Let's Talk Sense about Foreign Students." This describes a number of basic concerns so well that it should be read by everyone interested in the subject. Undoubtedly, insofar as students who study here are concerned, the basic question is what can they do with what they have learned when they return to their native lands? For if the answer should be "Nothing," the futility of the whole effort would have been demonstrated. Mr. Coombs said:

> For his own country and for ours the returned foreign student represents an important investment and asset. We know that in many, many individual instances these "assets" are put to highly productive use. The lists of what returned Fulbright scholars are doing to serve their fellowmen are most impressive.
>
> But there are many other cases in which the student returns home and fails to find a good opportunity to put his newly-gained skills and knowledge to good use, especially in the less-developed countries.
>
> There are many complex reasons for this and it is not a problem which can easily be solved. But it is vitally important that every effort be made to gain progress in this direction. . . .

These are observations of moment because they highlight one of the most complex areas of cultural exchange. On the one hand, it would be of interest and value to compare our experience with that of the French and the British, both of whom also have a considerable stake in helping post-colonial peoples to learn what perforce they must if their societies are to prosper. How, for example, would the British Commonwealth scholarship program compare with our Fulbright program in terms of the eventual contribution made by returning grantees? In theory it would seem that those in the British program should be more successful by reason of experience gained in the area. On the other hand, the question of what happens to students returning from the Soviet Union raises important and difficult questions of another character. If, as is perhaps to be assumed, the Russians continue to keep a watchful eye on young men and women who have studied in Moscow, and if indeed they do not fail actively to subsidize them, what questions would such actions present for the government of the United States?

We shall close with some comment on two problems which have been widely discussed, although the evidence concerning all of their implications may still be fragmentary. The first is the brain drain, that is, the siphoning off of workers, particularly in the applied sciences, not only from advanced countries like Great Britain and Germany but also from the developing countries which so seriously need them. Insofar as Europe is concerned the brain drain to the United States may to a great extent be compensated for by U.S. involvement in industry abroad and by readiness to assist in the development of centers of nuclear power for peaceful use. Certainly the import of brains by which we have most profited recently is that contributing to pure research in mathematics and the allied sciences. This is, however, only an addition to the great human resources made available to us as a result of the suppressive tyrannies which arose in Europe. Our gains have extended all the way from physics to art and music history. The situation in the underdeveloped countries is quite different in character and results primarily from inability to keep industrial development in step with educational advances. Able and well trained scholars returning from abroad find little scope for their efforts, and accept with little satisfaction the standard of living awaiting them. The temptation to re-settle abroad is understandably great.

The problem is complex and difficult, reflecting as perhaps no other situation does as clearly the vast differences in opportunity provided, for example, by the United States or by Germany and Eastern Europe.

The second problem arises out of the plain fact that cultural relations assume both in theory and in practice the universality of exchange. One may prefer to pool interests inside the familiar cultural terrain one has occupied with others, notably in this instance the countries of the West.

Indeed people used to speak of a "civilization of the Mediterranean," and to assume that this was so vastly superior to any other civilization that it was a waste of time to look elsewhere. But whatever may be tenable in the argument, it cannot have validity for us because we live in a time when the civilizations are converging. One may add parenthetically that at no period in its history has the West failed to profit from association with other civilizations, notably those of Islam and the East. Today we cannot afford to slice off any part of the world's heritage. The family of nations is not a name only but the sole conceivable prelude to peace. Accordingly, whatever the political, economic and ideological implications may be, cultural co-operation with China is indispensable.

What has been said may suffice to indicate that cultural relations are, insofar as the United States is concerned, at a stage of development which will require the very greatest intelligence and even venturesomeness, the term being admittedly new. I have employed it to symbolize what seems to me the key to the future, namely cautious but vigorous experimentation. The United States has come a long way. But it must move faster and farther. Perhaps in our planning for the future, we should also reckon with the tremendous increase of cultural relations activities which would take place if disarmament were in large measure achieved.

As of the time of writing it must be admitted that the outlook is disheartening. Another very able Assistant Secretary for Cultural Affairs has found it desirable to resign. Among the frustrations he was compelled to endure was the fact that the International Education Act, on which such high hopes had been placed, became only another scrap of paper, since no funds were allocated to support it. Moreover, sums for international research and exchange in humanistic studies appear to have virtually vanished. Finally "student power," always a problem in Latin America, has not only increased its strangle-hold on the universities but has taken on a coloring still more hostile to the United States than ever before. We can only hope that the climate generally will improve.

# 2. The Role of the Arts and the Humanities

## W. McNEIL LOWRY AND GERTRUDE S. HOOKER

The arts have never been the property of a whole nation or race, and something is risked when they are employed for social or political reasons. Ideally, intercultural mobility should emerge as a manifestation of the vitality, pervasiveness, and needs of the arts and the artists themselves, without reference to foreign policy, but in a society which at the same time sees the artist as a representative of some of its most conscious values. In sum, if we put this conception of the arts at the top of the scale and attempt to justify the expenditure of public funds, we must drop down through several philosophical levels before we come to the assumptions hitherto accepted for United States international cultural activities. From ideal to actual, the planes would arrange themselves as follows:

1. Spontaneous intercultural movement as a manifestation of the vitality and pervasiveness and needs of the arts and of the artist, without reference to foreign policy.

2. If such movement could not be spontaneous, but required public or private funds, then the use of such funds without reference to national foreign policies.

3. Public funds to use the arts as media by which to illuminate and reflect the Western ideal of the supremacy of the individual.

4. Public funds to reflect abroad a particularly American view of man, wherever it exists.

*The authors are indebted to Mrs. E. Ladd Thurston of Washington, D.C. for painstaking assistance in the revision of factual references in this chapter for the period 1962–67.*

Note that the arts are put at the top of the scale, and that even the last, the most constrained of the four objectives, does not assume that activities carried out to express it, can (in the language of the Fulbright-Hays Act) "assist in the development of friendly, sympathetic, and peaceful relations between the United States and other countries of the world." But why should the arts be put at the top of any scale when the subject is cultural activities and their relationship to United States foreign policy? The answers must here be given as short articles of faith.

One article is that what art is about is not what foreign policy is about. Art may easily suffer when it is used, as it often is, for non-artistic purposes. And if there is a question whether even good artistic exchange contributes to peace, and there is such a question, then perhaps we ought to assume that bad artistic exchange is not a good risk for United States foreign policy.

Another is that only when we begin with artistic considerations may we expect the support of the artists and artistic directors, and that without that support we again risk a bad exchange at both ends of the transaction. Art may or may not be mysterious, but the processes and techniques by which it is produced have often eluded the most powerful, the wealthiest, and the most determined men.

Indeed, there are direct corollaries between this intellectual argument and the ways in which the arts should be used in relation to foreign policy. We are concerned with *why* the arts are thus used; we must be equally concerned with *how*. And the point is that the farther we move from an ideal situation in which intercultural movements spontaneously manifest the vitality and the needs of the arts themselves, the more we need to cling to strictly artistic considerations when we are attempting to use the arts for other large purposes.

To keep artistic and political values most nearly in proper relation, government activities in the international cultural sphere should be managed directly and indirectly to:

1. Support art, the artist, and cultural activities for their own importance in society.

2. Use the strictest criteria of artistic excellence in the choice of artists and artistic groups employed; or

3. Employ those talented artists and artistic groups who will in the process be assisted in their professional development.

4. Help to improve public taste.

5. Profit from the intensive and realistic advice of artists and artistic directors themselves.

6. Ensure, by means of the above principles, the moral and intellectual support of the artistic community at home and abroad.

### PURPOSES OF CULTURAL EXCHANGE

Government-sponsored cultural activities overseas in the past have not been based upon artistic considerations and only partially upon general political motives such as upholding the idea of the supremacy of the individual. Instead, such activities have been based on the assumption they they would increase understanding and acceptance of United States policies and institutions.

When The American Assembly studied the question of cultural activities overseas in the symposium on *The Representation of the United States Abroad* in May, 1956, Mr. Howland Sargeant, former Assistant Secretary of State for Public Affairs, deplored the lack of "a clear, understandable United States government policy as to the role of these cultural relations in our national policy." In a brilliant exposition of information and cultural representation overseas—still largely valid—he resorted constantly to such adjectives as *muddy, complex, cloudy,* and *fuzzy* in trying to explain the relationship of cultural programs to foreign policy objectives as well as to the much more clear-cut information program.

A few weeks after he took office, President Kennedy called attention to the purposes of cultural and educational exchange programs when he observed that "the whole field was in need of imaginative policy direction, unification, and vigorous direction." A few months later, in September, 1961, passage of the new Fulbright-Hays Mutual Educational and Cultural Exchange Act invited and demanded a rethinking of the whole political and moral philosophy behind the programs.

The act itself defines the purposes of cultural exchange in very broad terms. It is intended to increase mutual understanding . . . , to strengthen the ties which unite us with other nations by demonstrating the educational and cultural interests, developments, and achievements of the people of the United States and other nations, and the contributions being made toward a peaceful and more fruitful life for people throughout the world; to promote international cooperation for educational and cultural advancement; and thus to assist in the development of friendly, sympathetic, and peaceful relations between the United States and other countries of the world.

Behind these unexceptionable intentions lay a whole cluster of more or less related and compatible purposes, but by 1967 they largely constituted only a statement of intent.

### Cultural competition among nations

Historically the United States was the last of the major nations to engage in government-sponsored cultural exchange, and its original motive was defensive. When the Division of Cultural Relations was established in the Department of State in 1938, its activity was limited to Latin America and its purpose was to counter Nazi and Fascist cultural propaganda in the Western hemisphere. Ever since, this negative approach has colored and often dominated official thinking and planning. When the Cold War has been intense, cultural diplomacy has been difficult to justify to the taxpayer except in terms of a contest or a race with the communists. The magnitude of the communist effort to reach the intellectuals has often obscured the fact that virtually all the advanced countries—no less than 49 in 1967 have cost-sharing educational agreements with the United States—carry on cultural and educational activities abroad as a routine part of foreign relations, for a great many reasons both idealistic and practical.

### "La mission civilisatrice"

The idea that cultural activities overseas have a "civilizing mission" has also traditionaly been quite alien to American (and British) thinking, and it is only recently that our responsibilities toward newly developing countries have raised the question with some urgency. Both British insularity and American isolationism, in their different ways, reflected a complacency about the excellence of their native institutions and way of life and the assumption that if other people did not wish to imitate us, so much the worse for them.

The French approach for many decades, or indeed centuries, has been very different. Herbert Lüthy traces the French missionary idea back to the Crusades and the noble Christian ideal of the *gesta Dei per Francos*. In any case, because France sees herself as the guardian of human civilization itself, she has at all times engaged in a dynamic campaign of "intellectual expansion" aimed, as we read in the 1960 Report of the Foreign Office, at offering other peoples, especially the young, the "formation" that comes with mastery of the logical and practical instrument that is the French language, and hence "the means of attaining a source of spiritual as well as material riches."

### The needs of newly developing countries

What the French have long known, and what we have only recently begun to recognize, is that there exists a large consumer demand for cultural commodities in other countries. Although this market is by no means limited to the less developed areas, its intentions are described with particular clarity by spokesmen for the new countries of tropical Africa. "Even when we have solved this problem (of colonialism)," wrote Leopold Senghor, "there will still be another problem—that of the choice between civilizations in contact; we shall have to see what we shall take from Western civilization and what we shall keep from Negro African civilization."

As the priority objectives of United States foreign policy have shifted from the postwar reconstruction of occupied countries through successive phases of the cold war to the present major concern with the growth of new and developing countries, cultural exchange has been called upon for a corresponding variety of contributions. In the early stages of the Point Four program its role was marginal, and limited to such matters as technical assistance in developing crafts as a resource for the local economy, or printed instructional materials. There seemed good reason to hope, especially with the Marshall Plan analogy in mind, that direct economic assistance along with precise technical training could give the necessary leverage to these countries, and do so in a short period.

It has become increasingly evident that simple economic betterment neither satisfies the aspirations of these peoples nor does it lead to the kind of "manageable instability" that is required for democratic institutions to evolve—in fact the appeal of the communists has been strongest in the field of material development. "Fortunately for us in terms of our competition with the communists," wrote Lloyd A. Free and Hadley Cantril in a report prepared in 1957 for the Rockefeller Brothers Fund:

> man is much more than an economic unit. It is not without signifi-
> cance, for example, that the strongest aspiration of all among former
> colonial peoples has been, not economic betterment, but political
> independence. Actually, the intensive nationalistic feelings of the
> people, even after they have won independence, have caused them
> frequently to act quite contrary to their own economic interests (as
> witness, for example, the Indonesians forcing out Dutch enterprises
> upon which the livelihood of many depended; the Burmese refusing
> the United States assistance they sorely needed; the Syrians sabotag-
> ing the pipelines upon which their national economy is dependent;
> the Jordanians renouncing a dependable British subsidy).
>
> In fact, economic betterment, alone and by itself, occurring within
> the framework now existing in many areas, may actually worsen the
> political situation and increase the danger of communist subversion,
> at least temporarily. By permitting the people to lift up their heads
> to new desires and aspirations, partial economic betterment may
> actually augment frustrations and discontent—unless it is accompa-
> nied by the poltical, social and psychological evolution in democratic
> directions necessary to give the people hope for the future founded
> upon confidence in their political, economic and social systems.

Among the non-economic needs of the new nations national cultural identity is a principal ingredient of politi-cal independence, and is often of very high significance. As Walter Laves has noted in his recent report on educa-tional exchange activities, "It sometimes represents the one national asset which establishes them on a footing of equal-ity with other countries, counterbalancing to some extent the economic and other deficiencies of which they are acutely aware."

## The needs of the American people

Just as the new countries are adding new dimensions to the meaning of cultural exchange, so the worldwide rapid pace of change made it logical for government cultural programs to contribute part of their resources to a better understanding of foreign cultures within the United States. This too is a revolutionary development.

The Fulbright-Hays Act is called the *Mutual* Educational and Cultural Exchange Act, and it makes possible a number of new reciprocal exchanges. It authorizes the use of government funds not only for bringing foreign creative and performing artists and athletes to the United States, but also for interchanges of handicrafts, books, translations and international expositions demonstrating cultural attainments, and other related purposes. But Congress has never appropriated funds for the "reverse flow" and the State Department has been specifically prohibited from using any money for this purpose, even though there are suggestive precedents in other countries.

France and Italy have long conducted cultural exchanges on the basis of reciprocal agreements, whereby art exhibits, for example, are exchanged, with each country paying the cost of the visiting exhibit within its own territory. Though the intention could be to share costs equally, the arrangement pleases and flatters other countries and no doubt contributes to the reputation of Paris as the world center of refined taste in the arts. The Soviet Union, in spite of withholding royalties, has for years won friends among foreign writers by translating their books systematically, often into several languages and usually long before other countries had discovered them, if indeed they ever did. Another example is that of the French-writing poet Leopold Senghor, who was published in Czechoslovakia in 1947, many years before he emerged as President of Senegal. It is not unlikely that this contributed to Senghor's pro-communist political views prior to the Hungarian revolution.

The International Educational and Cultural Exchange Program in the Department of State has, occasionally, acted as the middle man in aiding a country in making arrangements in the United States. Recently, the Dutch Government asked the State Department to facilitate the exchange of Rembrandt paintings with the Rijksmuseum. The National Gallery is prohibited from sending paintings abroad, but the Metropolitan Museum in New York willingly cooperated and an exchange was arranged. The large exhibitions in recent years at the National Gallery (one of Turkish treasures and one of Iranian art) have been successful, although somewhat embarrassing because the Gallery cannot reciprocate by sending American exhibitions abroad.

Increased understanding abroad of United States policies and institutions, cultural competition among nations, aid to the development of newly independent nations, better American understanding of foreign cultures—these have been the chief purposes upon which United States government activities were based until 1962. The passage of the Fulbright-Hays Act in 1961 led many persons to expect a more general, and less political, attention to cultural relations abroad. There is as yet no assurance of this development.

The American cultural resources used by public and private agencies overseas have chiefly been motivated by the objective of increased understanding of United States institutions and policies.

### UTILIZATION OF UNITED STATES CULTURAL RESOURCES

#### Musical arts and artists

In government exchange programs in the arts, musical artists have been the most active. From 1952 through 1966 the United States government awarded grants to some 2500 persons. (Since the number from 1952 to 1961 was 1189, it appears that the annual average has more than doubled, from 118 to 262.) Of these, 987 were foreign citizens coming to the United States and 1,313 were Americans who went abroad to continue their training. In addition, performers have travelled widely on government grants in music. Meanwhile young American singers continue to fill the opera houses of Germany and Italy with what has been evidently their richest source of supply.

The flow overseas of mature concert soloists has increased so notably in the last decade that artificial stimulus is usually unneccessary. The Department of State steps in only to extend commercial tours to countries or areas off the beaten concert path: for example, to send Eugene Istomin or Isaac Stern to Iceland, Rudolf Serkin to the Far East and India, Joseph Fuchs to Latin America and the Far East. A few concert artists in recent years began to reach tropical Africa: William Warfield pioneered in British West Africa in 1956, followed by Camilla Williams in 1958. In French tropical Africa the principal musical ambassadors have been Louis Armstrong, the Golden Gate Quartet, and the Westminster Singers. In the new countries the volume of musical traffic is limited not only by costs but sometimes by the lack of a suitable hall or even a piano. The roster of more recent concert engagements includes singers Adele Addison and Phyllis Curtin, pianists Malcolm Frager, Eugene Istomin and Ann Schein, and the classical harmonica virtuoso, John Sebastian.

American composers have also participated regularly in cultural exchange, and many of the major ones have been sent abroad by the government. Private foundations such as the Martha Baird Rockefeller Fund, the Guggenheim and the Rockefeller also provide opportunities for musical talent to work abroad. The American Academy in Rome gives hospitality to several young composers annually. Concerts organized by USIS provide recognition and experience for the young artists; USIS lectures and recorded concerts go on around the world, according to the energy and imagination of individual USIS officers.

If the musical artists, especially at the student level, have been conspicuous abroad, notably in Germany and Italy, overseas tours of American symphony orchestras are still a comparative rarity. The New York Philharmonic is the most widely traveled, having made European tours in 1955 and 1959, visited Latin America in 1958, Greece-Lebanon-Turkey in 1959, and Japan in 1961. The Los Angeles Symphony visited the Far East in 1956, Europe in 1963 and Eastern Europe and the Near East in 1966–67 as an extension of its world tour. Orchestras which have been more than once to Europe include the Philadelphia and the Cleveland. The Boston Symphony visited Europe in 1956 and the Far East in 1960. Latin America has been toured by the National, the Philadelphia and New Orleans symphonies; the Near East by the Minneapolis Symphony. The Pittsburgh Symphony toured extensively in Western Europe, Eastern Europe and the Near East in 1964.

The average cost to the Department of State of a Latin American tour by a symphony orchestra is $750,000 (an increase of 50% over comparable figures for 1962), or almost one-half of the cultural presentations program's $1,600,000 budget for 1967 (a decrease of 20% from 1962). At the present level of appropriations, it is impossible to send more than one orchestra a year, whereas formerly it was possible to send two with available funds. Thus even major foreign capitals are unlikely to have more than one concert by an American orchestra at intervals of several years.

Other very costly tours have been those of *Porgy and Bess* (1955), *Oklahoma* (1955) and *My Fair Lady* (USSR, 1960) and *Hello Dolly* (Japan, 1965). Two university musical comedy productions toured in 1962, the University of Utah's *Annie Get Your Gun* in Latin America and Southern Illinois University's *Born Yesterday* in Scotland. Until recently the high cost has ruled out opera altogether. In 1961, however, the Santa Fe Opera received limited assistance to perform at the Berlin Festival and in Belgrade: along with two Stravinsky works, it presented Douglas Moore's *Ballad of Baby Doe*. Otherwise foreign music lovers have had no opportunity to evaluate the condition of opera in the United States except marginally, e.g., at the Spoleto Festival, or through the performances of American singers on their own stages.

Mention should also be made of government-sponsored performances abroad of several chamber music ensembles and choral groups. Benny Goodman, the Robert Shaw Chorale and a number of other musical artists visited the USSR under the exchange agreement. In the summer of 1962 an American high school choir (from Princeton, New Jersey) went to Europe for the first time with partial government assistance. College choirs sponsored include Howard to Latin America (1960), Oberlin to Rumania and the USSR, and Peabody to the Far East, both in 1964.

Chamber music ensembles include the New York Woodwind Quintet, which toured Latin America (1956) and the Far East (1962) and the renowned Juilliard String Quartet, which toured in Europe and the Near East (1955), USSR (1965) and the Far East (1961 and 1966). Perhaps the group's most useful work was in two two-week workshops in 1966, one in Korea and the other in Japan, each attended enthusiastically by about five hundred students and faculty.

Other government programs involving music include the United States Specialists program (see below) and the various USIA media—collections of records and printed music, background lectures, documentary films such as *The Tanglewood Story, Design for Music,* others on Marian Anderson's tour of the Far and Near East and that of the Boston Symphony in Japan.

Examples of international musical exchange and cooperation under private initiative are too numerous to report in detail and have been multiplying in the last few years. The Tanglewood festival has imported major European figures fairly systematically for many years. There has been increased cooperation among European and American opera houses in sharing the cost of new sets. A number of American conductors have been working at intervals in the Far East, training orchestras and investigating the Oriental musical idioms. Examples might be multiplied.

*Some Results of Musical Exchanges*—This description suggests a great deal of activity, and probably musical artists are happier than their colleagues in other fields about the opportunities and the things that are happening to stimulate musical life. And yet, when the government resources are divided among 120 countries, it turns out that in many parts of the world American performing artists are rare indeed. USIS officers in Southeast Asia and Latin America, for example, report that American music is represented too often by second- or third-rate artists; composers complain that their works are virtually unknown abroad, even in Europe; another frequent comment is that too many grants go to young artists who could receive as good or better training in the United States, and should have it before they appear on European concert stages. It is also noted that the cultural presentations program is smaller than that of the British or the French, and that we have not systematically tried, as France does, to promote the works of native composers. Although United States government grantees are required to include some American music on their programs, composers note that the American number may be a very short one such as Barber's "Adagio for Strings."

Government-sponsored tours are run on exceedingly parsimonious budgets which have to be supplemented by private subsidies, ticket sales and so on. Commercial performances abroad rely on box office receipts to the maximum extent feasible, and the cost of tickets often discourages many music lovers.

Perhaps the most interesting by-products of postwar exchanges in music are seen in the contacts between Japan and the United States. In 1961 the East-West conference in Tokyo symbolized the fact that Japan is now one of the world's great cosmopolitan music centers; that it has a wealth of symphony orchestras (six in Tokyo alone) and an enviable supply of talented string players, a number of whom have won awards and acclaim in the United States. Later in 1961, following the visit of the Juilliard Quartet, plans were developed for a summer music camp in Japan, similar to those at Tanglewood and Marlboro, where young Japanese musicians (and perhaps those from other parts of Asia) might work with American teachers. In 1966 and 1967, two members of the Boston Symphony Orchestra, as a result of the Symphony's visit to Japan, exchanged with two Japanese musicians, members of the Japanese Philharmonic Orchestra. The respective orchestras paid salaries, the State Department paid travel expenses. Although there were no funds for families and the recipients were said to be in debt, the participants considered it a very fruitful exchange.

Among Americans who have been particularly active in disseminating knowledge of Indian music, the work of Alan Hovhaness, Howard Boatwright and William Malm has attracted particular attention. Mr. Boatwright recently published a textbook on the system he has devised for adapting Indian music to the Western five-line staff notation; Mr.

Malm is the author of *Japanese Music and Musical Instruments*. Meanwhile in the United States the University of California at Los Angeles has become a leading center of study and performance of the music of Japan, Indonesia, Iran, India and China, and held its first festival of Oriental Music and the Related Arts in 1960. The Ford and Rockefeller Foundations have supported this activity, to assist purchase of Asian and Latin American instruments and research materials as well as for study opportunities for Asian, Latin American and North American musicians.

### Theater

The condition of the American theater must be judged overseas almost exclusively by the plays and playwrights. Albee, Miller, Wilder, Williams, O'Neill—and all distinguished American playwrights—are not only household names among theatergoers abroad, but indeed victims of not infrequent unauthorized performances and pirated editions. In contrast to this lively circulation of leading American plays, the state of the American theater is otherwise impossible to appraise since so few companies have as yet attempted overseas tours. Paradoxically, the theater companies used to operating without funds are the only ones to have ventured abroad in the '60's—the La Mama troupe and the Living Theatre. The result has been that in Western and Eastern Europe, the American avant-garde playwrights (Melfi, von Itallie, Terry, etc.) are often better known than in the United States.

United States government efforts are still rudimentary. The first pilot project was sent out in 1956, when *Teahouse of the August Moon* toured five Latin American countries. The following year the Department of State made a major effort, but limited chiefly to Paris and the Théâtre des Nations, which was then in its first year. In connection with the "Salute to France" the Department partially subsidized performances of *Medea* with Judith Anderson, Wilder's *The Skin of Our Teeth,* and O'Neill's *Long Day's Journey into Night.* In 1961, more than a million dollars of the cultural presentations fund went to a quickly organized Theatre Guild American Repertory Company to present three contemporary plays: *The Skin of Our Teeth, The Glass*

*Menagerie,* and *The Miracle Worker.* This group, headed by Helen Hayes and Leif Ericson, visited 24 cities in Europe and the Near East, and another dozen in Latin America.

Since 1961, professional theater companies have not looked to government assistance with any real expectations for help in foreign tours. The advisory panel to the State Department's program has had to concentrate on other objectives, and the sense of frustration has been constant. Government sponsored tours have included university and other small groups or demonstration teams. In 1962 two university groups toured, Maine's Masquers Theatre and Montana State College's student team, both to the Far East. Utah visited Latin America in 1963, as had Catholic University in 1958. The latter made a tour of Europe and the Near East in 1965. In 1966 Ruth Brinkman's American Players, a small group, toured Northern Europe and Iceland, playing mostly to high school and college students in American studies programs.

If one contrasts this modest record with the annual theatrical manifestations abroad under French government auspices, the relative impact of American offerings appears to be slight and fleeting.

The most important international theater festival is the annual Théâtre des Nations, held every spring in Paris. The idea emerged from the 1955 meeting of the International Theatre Institute in Dubrovnik, and the Festival got underway in 1957. During the 1962 season 23 nations participated (as against 19 the year before) in 41 different performances, the largest program to date. Since its inception, the Théâtre des Nations has presented most of the world's greatest theater, from the Berliner Ensemble and the Berlin Opera, to the most distinguished companies of England, Italy, Ireland, Greece, the USSR and many others. United States participation has been haphazard, except for the first year.

Otherwise, United States activity in the theater has mainly been represented overseas by individuals. Under government exchange programs 528 Americans in theater arts have gone abroad to study, teach, or do research, and over 400 foreign grantees have come to this country (the number having doubled in the past five years). Fulbright grantees from American university theater departments have participated in or initiated theater seminars, readings or performances from Finland to India.

### Dance and ballet

Of all the performing arts other than concert music, ballet has been most adequately represented overseas. Three principal United States companies have toured abroad several times under the cultural presentations program: Lucia Chase's American Ballet Theatre, four tours, including Latin America, Europe, the Near East and Africa, from 1955 to 1960; the San Francisco Ballet, three tours, including the Far East, Near East, Latin America and Africa, from 1957 to 1959; and the New York City Center Ballet which went to Europe in 1956, the Far East in 1958, and the USSR and East and West Europe (fall, 1962). In 1959 Jerome Robbins' *Ballets USA* toured Europe, Poland, Yugoslavia, Israel and Greece arousing storms both of praise and criticism. In the dance field, Martha Graham toured the Far East and Near East in 1956; Jose Limon has appeared twice in Latin America and once in Europe and East Europe. No American ballet company has yet visited countries of central Africa, although the Bolshoi ballet has been there. In the 1960's Martha Graham's troupe toured Europe and the Near East in 1962 and England and Portugal in 1967. The Robert Joffrey Ballet visited the USSR and Near East in 1962, and in the same year the New York City Ballet toured Eastern Europe and the USSR. In 1965 it went to Europe and the Near East. The American Ballet Theatre went to Latin America in 1964 and to the USSR in 1966. Jose Limon toured again (1963) to the Far East. Paul Taylor's troupe went to Latin America in 1965 and the Far East in 1967. In 1967 Alvin Ailey also toured Africa with marked success.

### Visual arts, artists, exhibitions, museums

A paradoxical state of affairs emerges when one attempts to analyze what is happening overseas to American art and artists. On the one hand, of all the artists, it is the painters who have won the highest distinction on the international scene—recognition from Paris and London that the style of painting most in vogue in New York today is, or was until yesterday, the most exciting and influential in the world. On the other hand, organized government activity in the arts has been halting and spotty and capricious in the extreme.

The federal government's program of touring exhibitions got underway shortly after the Second World War. It ran almost immediately into a storm of criticism from many of the citizens' groups which in a democracy insist on monitoring all aspects of government activity. There is not space here to review the various chapters of the often dramatic and astonishing tale: suffice it to say that the government has been cautious, and sometimes paralyzed altogether. It is not surprising that USIA, which has responsibility for art exhibitions, has done a minimum of reporting on its activities. [In 1965 touring exhibitions were transferred to the Smithsonian Institution's National Collection of Fine Arts, giving the program greater freedom. Its two major tasks are circulating exhibitions geared to five or six countries and the American entries at large international competitions, including the Venice Biennale, the Sao Paulo Bienal and (in February, 1968) the first Indian Triennale.]

In spite of the obstacles, several fairly large exhibitions have gone abroad under government sponsorship, chiefly to Europe. Among these were the exhibition of 19th century American painting which toured various European countries; the collection of French paintings in American collections *De David à Toulouse-Lautrec*; another, *French Drawings From American Collections,* shown in Rotterdam and Paris; *Twentieth Century Italian Art from American Collections,* shown in Milan and Rome; and the recent exhibit of *American Painting of the Twentieth Century* sent to Moscow. During the year 1962, USIA had the *American Vanguard* exhibit—a collection of 88 contemporary paintings—in Yugoslavia, Austria, Germany and London; along with a very few small collections of paintings elsewhere (14 to Santiago, for example, for the Pan American Art Festival; and 5 to northern Europe). But the principal emphasis has been on graphic arts and prints, which are obviously less expensive to handle, less difficult to display, less controversial, as well as highly distinguished for intrinsic artistic merit. Recent exhibitions include a

John Marin retrospective, Sandpainting and Hand Crafts by Indians, graphic arts, a show of eleven "Pop" artists, an exhibition of U.S. art in Santiago, and contemporary textiles. An Archipenko show is in the planning stage for Eastern Europe (1968).

As is apparent, the government's own program has been minimal. USIA's budget for fiscal year 1962 allowed only $3,500 for Washington support of art exhibitions, for example, though actual expenditures were in the vicinity of $20,000. The National Collection of Fine Arts had about 32 exhibitions planned for 1967, ranging from the expensive Venice Biennale to "Children's Art from American Museum Classes," a handicrafts exhibition, a Whistler show, and an exhibition of contemporary constructions and sculpture, "The New Vein."

Responsibility for presenting American art overseas was carried by the Museum of Modern Art prior to 1965, with principal support from the Rockefeller Brothers Fund. For many years the Museum handled United States representation at the two major international biennials in Venice and Sao Paulo, where such artists as Pollock, Rothko, Marin, Shahn, Calder, Kline and others were brought to the attention of the world's leading art critics. In April, 1962, the Museum announced that it could no longer afford to sponsor these activities. It reported that its outlay for handling the last thirteen exhibitions had been some $265,000 plus an estimated $250,000 in curatorial time, use of museum space and the like. The current budget is roughly $100,000 and the Smithsonian has been able almost to double this amount through private contributions to defray the large cost of the biennals. Ideally Congress would appropriate funds explicitly for the biennals and the Smithsonian could cease fund raising for that effort. The large cost of shipping works to the recent Sao Paulo Bienal in Brazil was donated, as were the extensive and handsome catalogues. All of this was in addition to the funds needed for the exhibition.

In any event American art has continued to attract attention abroad, with Robert Rauschenberg winning the grand prize at Venice and Llyn Foulkes first prize at Paris (1964). In 1967 the American pavilion at Sao Paulo won a prize for its varied exhibition.

The combined resources of the American government

and private sponsors do not add up to those of other governments. Again looking at the French example, one notes that even in 1960 a total of forty-two art exhibitions, comprising 5,800 works of art, traveled abroad to eighteen countries. In selecting works for export, special emphasis was placed on contemporary painting, sculpture, printmaking, tapestry and decorative arts.

A number of efforts are being made apart from touring exhibitions. Among these is the collection of 2,500 slides on American arts and crafts assembled with assistance from the Carnegie Corporation and designed in part for deposit in libraries and institutions abroad. The Ford Foundation is currently supporting a series of monographs on living American artists intended for dissemination overseas as well as in the United States. Another Ford program is assisting American art museums in the preparation of annotated catalogues of their collections—a need that has often been stressed by art critics and connoisseurs abroad. USIA over the years has subsidized translations of books such as John Baur's *Revolution and Tradition in American Art*; it has promoted diffusion of French and Italian editions of *New Art in America,* and occasionally presented other art books to institutions. An imaginative pilot project set up recently by the Museum of Modern Art provides outstanding works of art for ambassadors' residences abroad on a circulating loan basis. For the last six years, the privately sponsored Woodward Foundation program has lent prints and paintings from its collection to American ambassadors abroad for their residences and offices. USIA has continued to circulate original prints in groups, to be used as travelling exhibitions and also hung in libraries and offices.

Some 1,100 Americans have received government grants in the last fifteen years (the number having nearly doubled in the past five years) to study and work abroad in painting, sculpture and the history of art; another 682 foreign artists and art historians came to the United States. The majority of these awards have gone to persons concerned with art history and scholarship rather than to creative painters and sculptors. A number of former Fulbright grantees in painting and sculpture have, however, won major honors.

Among institutions participating regularly in intercultural exchange, the Smithsonian Traveling Exhibition Service has been active since 1952 and handles most of the foreign exhibits in the United States, usually in cooperation with the embassy concerned. The American Association of Museums carries out a small but growing international program. In 1960, with State Department assistance, it organized the first of its annual regional tours for invited foreign professionals (10 in 1960, 17 in 1961 and again in 1962), who subsequently attend the annual meeting of the AAM and have an opportunity to meet colleagues from all parts of the United States and Canada.

Private foundations have also recently begun to make small but growing grants for the development of the arts, crafts and museums in lesser developed countries.

### The humanities

Contacts between humanists in the United States and those in other countries since the Second World War have been numerous, but less organized, than contacts in other fields. Except for American studies, United States government support has been limited and spasmodic. Through the senior Fulbright appointments, many American humanists have spent some time abroad, chiefly in the fields of history and literature. Many more have traveled under grants from foundations.

One of the major postwar academic developments has been the organization of area studies, especially those relating to Soviet Russia, the Near East, Southeast Asia, the Far East, Africa and Latin America. Many American scholars have traveled and studied abroad in connection with these programs, a few with government support but the great majority under grants from the Ford, Rockefeller, and other foundations. In numerous instances these grants have been made by the American Council of Learned Societies, the Social Sciences Research Council or by universities themselves, but the funds for these grants have come chiefly from the sources mentioned.

At the same time, the United States has made many contributions to the studies of these areas in foreign countries, again chiefly through grants by the Rockefeller, Carnegie, and Ford Foundations. The conclusions of the Scarborough

Commission providing for university support of area studies
in the United Kingdom were reached after travel of members of the Commission in the United States under the auspices of the Rockefeller Foundation. The large program of
area studies of the 6th Section, École Pratique des Hautes
Études, Paris, followed visits to the United States by Professor Fernand Braudel and several colleagues under
Rockefeller Foundation grants. The support of area studies
at Nuffield College and St. Anthony's College in Oxford
owes much to the Ford and Rockefeller Foundations. Similarly, Soviet and Chinese studies in Japan were aided by
fellowships and travel grants of the Rockefeller Foundation. A number of Ford Foundation grants for African
studies, in tropical Africa as well as in the United States,
have potential political as well as cultural significance.

Contacts in other fields of the humanities, notably linguistics and philosophy, have been frequent, although not
usually systematic. The spread of English as a second language (to which foundations as well as the government have
contributed many millions) and the study of descriptive
linguistics, are responsible for many contacts involving
scholars from Egypt, India, the Philippines, and Latin
America.

In 1958 The Ford Foundation granted funds to the
American Council of Learned Societies and the Social
Sciences Research Council for a program to encourage international scholarly congresses in the humanities and social
sciences to meet in the United States. At that time only one
international congress of special concern to the ACLS and
SSRC membership had met in the United States since
World War II; since then American scholars have been able
to play host to their foreign colleagues in musicology and
history of art (1961) and in sociology and history of science
(1962); in the plastic arts and medieval canon law (1963) and
in the history of religion and in problems of urbanization
(1965). The International Council of Museums met in New
York in 1965; in the same year the International Study
Group on Political Finance met in Washington. The International PEN, representing writers from all over the world,
and the International Theatre Institute met in the United
States in 1967, with programs both in New York City and
elsewhere.

The most extensive programs involving foreign scholars have been those in American studies, supported both by private and governmental funds. The term "American studies" is still in need of a clear definition at home and is often equated with an interdisciplinary approach typical of area studies in general; but in the intention of the few persons in the Department of State, USIS and certain foundations who have been working to encourage American studies, what is meant is university-level study of American history, literature, fine arts, and political institutions on a par with the formal attention given to these disciplines of other countries. At this early stage, American history is the field which needs the most attention just as it has been the most neglected by foreign historians, with few exceptions. Here one encounters the massive opposition of the traditional European approach to education, whereby the entire field of twentieth century history is almost ruled out, and American history is only an incidental casualty—notably the case in France, where the "fifty-year rule" keeps students of history from access to any archives after 1918.

In spite of such obstacles, the number of courses in American history and literature given overseas in the last decade has been steadily increasing, and a movement which started in Western Europe had spread by 1960 throughout most of the world, with courses in history as well as literature being offered in India, Japan, Peru, Pakistan, Iran, Argentina, etc. The Salzburg Seminar, also with foundation support, has long provided another stimulus to younger scholars through intensive one-month seminars.

In 1960 The Ford Foundation began its support of a program of the American Council of Learned Societies for the encouragement of American studies in Europe, and this may contribute significantly to solving such problems as the need for course materials and travel and study opportunities for the slowly growing nucleus of mature scholars who are doing specialized work on American institutions, thought and history. It is not yet certain whether American scholarly interests will be able vigorously to attack what has been and still is the principal barrier for European scholars interested in American studies: the lack of adequate research materials and of a great research library in the field, somewhere on the continent. Although books and overseas libraries have received a great deal of attention on the part of both government and private initiative, as we shall now see, the central problem—by no means insoluble—remains to be faced.

### Overseas libraries

Books and libraries are at the heart of government cultural programs overseas, just as the library is the focal point of the cultural or information center. In 1967 USIA had reduced its operation to 159 information centers operating in 85 countries, supplemented by another 63 reading rooms and small book collections; whereas in 1961 there had been 181 information centers and 85 reading rooms and small book collections. In addition, another 130 binational centers instead of 145 previously, chiefly in Latin America, contained collections of books and periodicals. Most of the USIS libraries average 10-15,000 volumes, although they range in size from the Berlin Amerika Haus, with more than 50,000 volumes, to the 1,200 volume basic collections in new libraries in Africa.

The USIS library is usually the chief or the only source of American books overseas for the average reader and even for most university students. Only in Paris is there an important private American library, open to the general public, but it is small by the standards of an American university library. USIS libraries consist largely of current books and periodicals and government publications, along with translations of American books into local languages, wherever available.

For several decades American foundations have made grants to foreign universities and libraries for the purchase of collections of American books. In spite of these continuing efforts, the demand seems to be inexhaustible. USIS too has made presentations to institutions—chiefly books on American literature, history and culture—but at no time have funds for this purpose (always vulnerable in Congressional eyes) been adequate to allow for more than token activities. In the last few years they have declined to a world wide total of $140,752 (1967 estimate) for presentations both to individuals and institutions. Some of the university contracts of the Agency for International Development (formerly the International Cooperation Administration) have included funds for initial gifts of books for specialized subjects in the relevant field. In India, for a few years, the Wheat Loan bill made it possible to purchase annually about $500,000 in books for Indian libraries. Finally, numerous private organizations and individuals have provided voluntary books and services, from CARE and the well-established United States Book Exchange to the sporadic and often counterproductive efforts of citizens' book drives across the country.

### Sales of American books overseas

It is difficult to obtain reliable facts or even opinions about the availability of American books in bookstores overseas. By 1963 export of books and printed materials had multiplied ten times since the Second World War, more than that of any other country. The development of the paperback industry has obviously increased the market for good paperbacks as well as the others. But the United States publishing industry, unlike the British and the French, has not been either proficient or greatly interested in the export market, and even in most European countries professors and scholars who know what book they want have to order it from the United States.

The United States government tried to remedy this problem, wherever dollar shortages were the cause, through the Informational Media Guaranty Program. Since its inception in 1948 as part of the European Recovery Program to the ending of the program in 1967, it was generally acclaimed and was a model for similar schemes of other governments. Many publishers have deplored the fact that the IMG program has ceased. USIA, which administered the program, last received appropriations in 1964 but continued operating on the turnover of funds until liquidation in 1967. At its beginning 55% of the IMG contracts were with book publishers, with magazine publishers receiving 20%, motion picture producers 22%, and miscellaneous printed materials such as maps 3%. Later a higher percentage went to book publishers, and there was stronger emphasis on text and reference books of a scientific and educational character, though these already received 41% of

IMG contracts. English-teaching texts received first priority when the program ceased.

*USIA Book Programs*—Since 1950 USIA has promoted the translation and distribution of books "which illustrate important aspects of American life or culture or which contribute significantly to U.S. foreign policy objectives." By June, 1967, some 15,162 editions had been published in 56 languages, totalling about 134 million copies.

Student editions, in English reprints of paperback selling for twenty cents, totalled 36 editions and 782,801 copies by mid-1967. Undertaken ten years earlier, primarily to meet the needs in the Near East and Far East, student editions are exact reprints of books on American art, biography, fiction, government, history, medicine, and science.

Simplified editions selling for fifteen cents, the "Ladder" series, are designed for neo-literates in English and include books of the same general type as the student editions but with basic vocabularies of from one to five thousand words. USIA produces 52 titles of the "Ladder" series in French for countries of tropical Africa.

In 1962, USIA initiated a low-priced book translation program, based in Paris, translating into French short American books or condensed versions, for African consumption. Retailing for twenty to thirty cents, many of these books are also distributed in Vietnam, Laos and Cambodia. By the middle of 1966 about 340 editions had been published. In Latin America by the same date, 434 editions in 4,400,000 copies had come out in Spanish and Portuguese, and in India the Book Translation Program had brought out 422 editions in 1,900,000 copies in a total of thirteen languages.

USIA utilizes foreign currencies accruing from the sale of surplus agricultural commodities under the Agricultural Trade Development and Assistance Act of 1954 (Public Law 480, 83rd Congress) to finance "the translation, publication and distribution of books and periodicals, including government publications, abroad." By the end of 1960 currencies were available in 22 of the 26 countries with which bilateral agreements had been signed and textbook programs were underway. By May, 1962, 53 titles had been published in 12 languages in 13 countries, chiefly scientific textbooks, although in France and Italy textbooks in the humanities—especially history and political science—were predominant. In Italy 15 volumes of a 20-volume series of "Classics of Western Democracy" had appeared. By mid-1966 the program was still in operation in 15 countries. The largest program, the Indian, produced 153 English reprints, primarily in the natural and applied sciences. Ninety per cent of these are assigned in one or more of India's 63 universities, and some have been adopted by over 50 universities or colleges. Of the other large programs, that in the United Arab Republic is currently suspended; the Yugoslav produces 39 titles in 136,500 copies. The Polish program started in 1965 produced three translated medical textbooks, in 8,000 editions, by mid-1967.

The USIA now circulates book exhibits, produced cooperatively with American publishers. Emphasis is given to low-priced paperbacks. Currently "The World of Paperbacks," a listing of 900 to 1,200 titles in 15 sets, is circulating to 44 countries. "Science and Technology," seven to ten sets of as many as 800 titles is visiting 28 countries, and "Teaching of English as a Foreign Language," in 16 sets, is due to travel in early 1968. The publishers provide the books to be sold at standard prices. The USIA schedules the exhibitions abroad, ships the books and shows them at universities and book fairs.

Starting in June, 1952, Franklin Publications assisted the publication of additional books, chiefly in Arabic and Persian, but with a growing output in Urdu, Bengali, Malay, Indonesian and the Pushtu language of Afghanistan. As a non-profit private corporation, Franklin received financial support from foundations, corporations, individuals and governments (United States and other). With its headquarters in New York it worked closely with the publishing industry, notably in providing technical assistance in the development of a strong local book industry. Since the beginning, Franklin stressed its reliance on local initiative and support, official and professional, and it has enjoyed other advantages of continuity. A check of titles published indicates that they are generally identical with books supported by USIA in similar areas, with the exception of a few long-term and costly projects such as a Persian dictionary, supported by The Ford Foundation, an English-Arabic dictionary assisted by the Rockefeller Foundation, and translations into five languages of the *Columbia-Viking Desk Encyclopedia,* with assistance from various sources.

## "Reverse flow" translation programs

In the recent past there has been growing awareness of the need to make more of the literature and thought of other countries available in the United States. In 1952 the Rockefeller Foundation made a first grant to the Modern Language Association for an inquiry into the role that foreign languages and literature should play in American life. In 1959 the Rockefeller Brothers Fund initiated a program for translations from the literatures of Asia being carried out by the Asia Society. In 1962 the Rockefeller Foundation made a similar important grant to the Association of American University Presses for encouragement of translations of Latin American writings, and in 1964 The Ford Foundation established The National Translation Center at Austin, Texas, with an initial grant of $750,000.

These combined efforts do not match activities in publishing and translation in the Soviet Union, which have become so astronomical as to defy interpretation. One reliable source reports that 40 million books in foreign languages were published in 1960 largely for distribution in the underdeveloped countries. Included were textbooks strictly devoid of political content, books for children, a number of works of contemporary Soviet novelists, along with Marxist classics. The most frequent languages were English, French, Spanish, Arabic, Hindi and Bengali in that order. In addition to translations exported from the USSR, an additional Soviet publishing effort goes on in many countries locally, of substantial if unknown proportions.

## Proposals for increasing the flow of books

In the face of all the pressures, it was universally agreed that both government and private achievements to date had fallen far short of needs and responsibilities. When a State Department task force met in June, 1961, twenty-seven discrete proposals were made. "One of the most important problems of all," wrote one highly experienced observer, "is the integration of activity within the United States. One problem has been that we have literally dozens of programs dealing with American books overseas. . . . There is little coordination among these activities." Even among the principal government agencies involved, he added, there is an evident discrepancy in purpose and policy. "The people who have been most active in the use of books—the USIA—have seen them as instruments of persuasion rather than as tools of development. The people concerned with economic development have thought of books only marginally and if they have used them at all have done so for only temporary projects. There has been no concentrated planning." This comment, one might add, takes into account only two of the purposes of books as an instrument for cultural exchange. To rectify this situation a Government Advisory Committee on International Book and Library Programs was established in October, 1962, by the Secretary of State, to advise the government on the policies and operations of its overseas book and library programs and to achieve closer coordination between public and private book and library activities overseas. The members (publishers, educators and one librarian) meet with government representatives from State, USIA and AID. The Committee recommended formation of the Interagency Book Committee, which is now the central place within government to implement action. In 1966 the Committee formulated a national policy statement on international book and library activities which the President approved in January, 1967.

Of all the resources at our disposal, books are surely the most precise and eloquent instrument of all. In many ways, they are the least costly and most enduring of the communications media. To date our utilization of books, and significant periodical literature, is still rudimentary. The government effort appears increasingly directed toward neo-literates and the use of books as a tool for development. Commercial exporters are primarily concerned with subliterary products for a universal public interested in entertainment. No sustained effort is yet meeting the needs of the international intellectual community on whose solidarity real understanding depends, and for which books are the most vital need of all.

## Problems and Opportunities

The foregoing pages have shown some of the principal examples of exchanges in the arts and the humanities over the past decade or so—a substantial amount of activity which nonetheless falls well below the optimum in both quantity and quality. The one truly positive development in these years has been the growing public and congressional support. This enlarged base of support has been strongly assisted by the now considerable reservoir of former exchangees and cultural emissaries, government and private, who have experienced the stimulation and challenge of direct contact with other cultures, who have sensed the failure of communication and its intrinsic significance. A great deal of re-evaluation has been going on in an effort to sort out the resources and liabilities of the United States, to find out how these look to others and to ourselves, and to keep up with change which has been remarkably accelerated at home as elsewhere.

There is, of course, one overwhelming influence upon U.S. activities abroad, of which the strictly cultural is only a minor component. That influence is U.S. engagement in the Vietnam war. While it continues it influences attitudes toward the United States not only in Asia but world wide. In intellectual and artistic circles, whether in countries traditionally hostile or friendly to American interest, it is used to characterize all of American life. While U.S. involvement in Vietnam continues, it colors all the principles that could form a basis for argument. It is the authors' hope that a few general assumptions can nevertheless be stated at this point, so far as problems and opportunities for U.S. cultural exchange are concerned.

The first peculiarly American liability in cultural exchange is thus, paradoxically, an asset. That is the very fundamental handicap of the confused and contradictory state of American critical opinion as to the merits and defects of American culture. If there are identifiable, purely American artifacts and institutions, which are they? What is the national character, the "national style"? When foreign observers try to isolate what is specifically American in the amalgam, they fall back on the American Indian, with jazz, the Negro problem, racial discrimination and alleged "imperialism" also coming at once into focus. American critics may go to the other extreme and find European sources so recondite and pervasive that little identity remains.

But it is also an advantage that American culture is a product of the entire Western heritage. It should be possible to communicate in many different artistic and intellectual idioms. The process of assimilating and importing the best of European and other cultures has been intense since the mid-thirties, with few interruptions. In all artistic fields (except creative literature) the flow of foreign talent to the United States, especially to New York, has probably been unequaled in any other major capital.

Another resource which the United States possesses in unprecedented abundance is the whole apparatus of communications media and techniques: the English language to start with, the techniques for mass production of cultural materials and especially for distributing them, and above all the mentality which assumes that it is desirable and profitable to reach as many consumers as possible. We are in a position, at least potentially, to export or re-export the best products available.

The rapid spread of English in the postwar period has been a surprising phenomenon, which originally was not officially contemplated or fostered. To be sure, the British Council has long recognized the central importance of language teaching, just as France has always been equally clear about the key significance of the French language as an introduction to French civilization and influence. But the United States has been caught short by the spread of English, and government English-teaching programs overseas are only now "tooling up," amid a critical shortage of teachers. The demand for reading materials and films seems inexhaustible and is so obvious that for the past decade the Soviet Union has also been publishing extensively in English.

Language is an asset of unprecedented potentiality; it also entails heavy responsibilities. Countless observers, foreign and American, are concerned about the nature of the "unprogrammed" exports from the United States, in English, and opinions are often apocalyptic. We may know less than we thought we did about the ultimate psychological impact of these offshoots of popular culture on overseas consumers who are not intellectuals, as their American consumers are not. In any case, until the Vietnam adventure at any rate, most of the myths and prejudices about American culture overseas were to be traced to foreign intellectuals who, we assume, are not the consumers of these products of mass media.

### Bureaucratic difficulties

One generalization made is that the resources of our communications machinery—government and private—have not been used to their full capacity for exporting the *best* products of United States and Western thought and culture. Virtually every commentator on government programs stresses the recurring need to keep quality in mind, as do innumerable field officers concerned with cultural affairs. Obviously many factors which militate against this goal are endemic in government operations and well known: the haphazard origin and financing of many programs, irresistible pressures to spread resources too thin, the impossibility of long-term planning on the basis of one-year appropriations, the confusion of purpose which results when these programs attempt to serve simultaneously all foreign policy objectives, the inevitable shifts of emphasis that accompany the constant movement of foreign service personnel, and so on.

In addition to, or perhaps because of, these conflicting influences, USIS operations overseas have since about 1955 been markedly decentralized. The policy was intended to encourage superior quality through closer cooperation with local populations and sensitivity to their needs, but the disadvantages have now begun to impress various observers. Just as American business overseas has recently been shifting to a policy of "recentralization," so a recent Report of the United States Advisory Commission on Information recommended that "communications within the Agency, presently weak, should be better both in Washington and in the field and between Washington and the field. Overseas personnel report that they feel themselves increasingly isolated from Washington." The ineffectiveness or inactivity of the various advisory committees concerned with arts and letters stems at least in part, in the view of some observers, from their lack of authority or influence. Although too much centralization and "masterminding" is also undesirable, and may be the more normal danger in a large bureaucracy, nonetheless the very broad mandate of a government cultural exchange program permits a most heterogeneous assortment of activities—unless there is constant evaluation of what is worth while and what is activity for the sake of activity. The USIA policy of decentralization assumes that the Public Affairs Officer knows best what is best for his area, and he has great latitude (subject, of course, to the approval of the ambassador). But in reality many Public Affairs Officers come from a background in journalism or radio and do not pretend to be able to evaluate events in the artistic and intellectual world, unless in terms of press coverage. On the other hand, many Cultural Affairs Officers feel the need for critical guidance, especially after several years overseas, and deplore the fact that they have to "be brilliant improvisers," as one officer put it. The advice should come, of course, from the most competent intellectual and artistic leadership in the United States.

### The complexities of the task abroad

If discontent at home is not lacking, there is of course a good deal of evidence from overseas that the prestige of American thought and culture—and hence of its capacity for leadership—has actually been lower in the last few years than it was fifteen or twenty years ago.

The case of France is a sufficiently painful if fortunately not completely typical one. It was acute even before the recent extravagances of General DeGaulle and the impact of U.S. engagement in Vietnam. To be sure, the whole matter of the "image" of the United States among foreign intellectuals is an exceedingly complex one and has to be traced back in France well over a century. Collaborative studies by an American and a French scholar, Durand Echeverria and René Remond, seem to prove that the last

American who was really esteemed in France was Benjamin Franklin, and the last French writer who looked at the United States with fresh eyes was de Tocqueville—who is hardly known among French university students. (The Rockefeller Foundation has prompted publication of a complete edition of his works, now finally slowly appearing.)

To some extent the alleged permanent immaturity and violence of American culture is a French and European literary theme with a long lineage which may survive indefinitely. But along with the burden of the past which cannot be removed in any case, some friendly European observers feel that the United States has been exporting too much of the wrong kind of information about herself suddenly of late, after so many decades when the image was schematic and haphazard. "In recent times there has increasingly been too much information, often contradictory, of unequal reliability, from many sources," wrote Julian Marias in *Foreign Affairs* (July 1961). But all this information and especially statistics—of which the United States compiles and exports a prodigious supply—in his view does not have the same meaning for foreigners because they start with quite different assumptions: "Unless there is a common assumption, language, instead of providing real communication, is misleading."

What is needed in order to bring the assumption into closer alignment, according to Mr. Marias, is "background and perspective." It will not suffice to give "the last-minute developments in politics, the last week's economic data, the monthly progress in integration" in order to change the "image of the United States as an intellectual wasteland and of American writers, artists and thinkers as exiles in their own country which . . . is almost uncontested in European intellectual circles today."

In an earlier essay in the book *As Others See Us: The United States through Foreign Eyes* (1959) this same observer explained more fully why he thinks misconceptions about the place of the artist and intellectual in American society are at the heart of anti-American prejudices:

> . . . there is a dominant assumption in Europe today that "the American" represents only a modification, an amplification—many people would say a corruption—of "the European." Implied here is

a lack of *originality* of the United States, an incapacity for *creation*. This in turn implies—and the assumption is widely held—monotony, vulgarity, "colossalism," intellectual inferiority. In certain respects the greatness of the United States is undeniable and is not denied, or at least infrequently. But this is understood to be merely a quantitative greatness and so suggests nothing really new or compelling. At most the United States is viewed as the country of the masses, where the superior individual has no role and rarely exists; the intellectual or the artist, be he American or foreign, is always an exile there, lost in a strange land of Philistines.

Obviously—as other friendly European critics note—the literary sources of these European assumptions are often native and the tradition of angry self-criticism from Mark Twain or Mencken to C. Wright Mills is long and articulate. But somehow there seems to be an insatiable appetite abroad for this fare. In part, as Raymond Aron and Martin Cunliffe note, malice and envy enter the picture, along with communist propaganda. But still other factors are involved.

There is some evidence that the way our cultural exchange programs have been working has involuntarily served to foster the idea that the arts and the humanities have little place in American education and values. The late Robert Blum noted that of the Asian students enrolled in American universities only about one-third are in the humanities and the social sciences; the majority specialize in engineering, medical, physical and natural sciences, agriculture, business administration and education. Although, in part, this reflects the shortage of technicians and specialists, there is also in play the Asian attitude toward American education, "which is often looked upon as being suitable in fields of practical study, but irrelevant or deficient where general ideas regarding society, history, philosophy, literature, and government are concerned. . . . This attitude was, and continues to be, nurtured by the British and French. . . ." What is true of the Asian students is largely valid for the entire foreign student body: of nearly 50,000 foreign students in the United States in 1959–60, less than 10,000 were studying the humanities and the arts.

There appears to be a vicious circle. The majority of foreign students come to the United States with the preconception that artistic and humanistic values will not be found, and then they arrange their study programs so as to avoid any exposure to these fields, should they exist.

Meanwhile, what of the role of the creative artist in other exchange programs? Are mature American artists and creative persons being utilized to an extent commensurate with their actual role in American society? A recent Department of State report shows that in the year ending in mid-1966, 338 Americans had grants in the arts of the total of 2,405 grantees, and foreign grantees numbered 334 of the 8,158 coming here. This includes a high percentage of persons from the teaching profession—some of whom are primarily creative artists but many of whom are not.

The only non-academic government program which sends Americans overseas for cultural purposes other than teaching, study or research, is the American Specialists Program. Since 1950 when it started, about 3,342 Americans annually have received full or partial Smith-Mundt grants for overseas visits, averaging thirty to ninety days. As conceived originally, this would seem to be the ideal opportunity for creative persons; and in fact a number of distinguished representatives have participated in it over the years—such writers as Katherine Anne Porter, William Faulkner, Allen Tate, Carl Sandburg and more recently John Steinbeck, John Cheever, John Updike, and Edward Albee. But in reality their visits have usually been fleeting, even in European countries. For years USIS cultural officers have been deploring the fact that so few distinguished lecturers and representatives came their way.

Many factors conspire to impede full utilization of the American Specialists Program in behalf of the artistic and intellectual community. In countries where there has been no Fulbright program, these Smith-Mundt funds have had to fill needs for teaching personnel, usually for periods much longer than ninety days, at high cost. In a recent Olympic year, over twenty per cent of the grants were used to meet field requests for professional athletic coaches to train local participants in the Olympic games. In general, the American Specialists Program has been a catch-all for all the miscellaneous travel grants requested by overseas posts to carry out seminars, clinics, workshops, and exhibits in a variety of subjects ranging from plastics to puppetry.

In commenting on this program Professor Laves recommends that there should be a highly qualified staff in Washington in a position to "develop a substantial reservoir of 'prestige' participants representing the top strata of American professional life," but the problem seems really to have lain with the administrative organization, which placed responsibility for planning with the field posts. A number of distinguished writers found that when they offered their services, it was difficult for government officials to reach a decision because the field posts had to be consulted.

It is true that this review does not take into account an indefinite number of cultural representatives who travel on their own initiative, with sabbatical leaves or private resources. And yet it is difficult to escape the conclusion that the total American effort has been modest and haphazard, especially compared with that of other governments. Statistics from the USSR may be inflated, but they suggest a different emphasis on these activities.

The British Council also gives a high priority to what it calls "Specialist Tours, Advisory Visits and Delegations." "Our main task," wrote the Director-General recently in the 21st Anniversary Report, "is the making and fostering of contacts between individual people. We have not the resources, even if the attempt were desirable, to make any direct impact on the masses." Selection of individuals to go overseas is made by the various Advisory Committees and Panels which work closely with the Council staff in all activities.

### The arts and area priorities

Ever since the beginning of United States government cultural exchange there has been a running debate as to whether these activities can or should conform to the objectives of foreign policy; and if so, whether to long- or short-range goals. In the case of the information programs, no such question exists. The fact that the two activities are merged overseas under the single administration of USIA has provided the appearance of a solution, or at least a truce, but a civil war has gone on steadily between those who seek immediate and spectacular success and those who believe cultural exchange should proceed quietly and steadily but with a few modest long-range ends hopefully in view.

But whichever position one takes—and in recent years partisans on both sides seem to have been about equally divided—neither point of view provides an automatic solution to the question of area priorities.

If this were an ideal world where it was unnecessary to think about politics, one might conclude that the universal language of the arts has a universal appeal and it is impossible to decide whether it matters more to the Japanese or the Brazilians or the Senegalese. In different ways, but with unanimous insistence, each area and country, with few exceptions, claims its own stake in the arts—and a need and a right to find self-expression and self-identity in its own writers and artists.

Most people agree with Northrup that the civilization of East Asia can be characterized as aesthetic in contrast to the theoretic and logical approach of the West. Former Ambassador Reischauer in his writings on Japan has called attention to the extent to which the arts—especially poetry and the graphic arts—have permeated Japanese life as a whole. For example: national poetry contests are not unusual, and even successful politicians are expected to be able to compose poems as well as speeches. Even in music, in which they had long lagged behind, the Japanese have recently shown the same kind of prowess in mastering the technique of playing the most difficult Western string instruments that marked their mastery of the refined art of Chinese prints in the nineteenth century. East Asia and especially Japan have many claims to very high area priority in cultural exchange.

In Latin America, where concern with cultural matters is restricted to a still small elite, the most informed observers warn that the political authority of these creative intellectuals cannot be over-estimated. Salvador de Madariaga's views as expressed in the *Saturday Review* (March 25, 1961) are typical:

> In Latin America, however, a man may be writing poetry on Friday and become President or Minister of Foreign Affairs the following Sunday. Nor should one suppose that this phenomenon is limited to that form of power which derives from actual political functions. It

cannot be doubted, for instance, that the high reputation which Pablo Neruda enjoys as a poet considerably enhances his power over Chilean public opinion as a Communist leader.

No more grievous mistake could therefore be made by the public opinion of the United States than to shrug its shoulders at the pro-Soviet and anti-American wave that is sweeping intellectual circles in Latin America. From the ranks of these pink professors, poets, doctors, and lawyers, the men will be recruited who will actually govern Latin America not merely ten years hence, but maybe next year, maybe next month. The issue is immediate and urgent; and we must waste no time in facing it.

If one turns to the new countries of Africa, it is increasingly evident that in the thinking of their own leaders, cultural development is a primary and immediate need, for reasons both psychological and political. In the thinking of some of the most enlightened African leaders, the goal is not merely cultural development as a source of national identity and national pride, but also as a field in which regional cooperation can foster economic and political trends toward unification. However, it is not clear that the type of cultural assistance and development they need today can be supplied by routine USIS installations. Beginning in 1960 USIA began to open large new posts in tropical Africa. This experiment does not seem to have the general approval of political officers in the area, who question the need for USIS staffs as large as those of the State Department.

The cultural exchange program that the United States has had in most years with the countries of the Soviet bloc seems to be the most striking practical demonstration to date of the *political* usefulness of such contacts. Obviously it is too soon to draw far-reaching conclusions; and yet in the first three years after the first exchange agreement went into effect a small handful of artists, humanists and scholars managed to make the images the two peoples have of each other more complex and perhaps without Vietnam would have made it more difficult for the cold war to return in quite its former monolithic shape.

It may be true—we do not know—that there is less need for government "information" programs in Europe than there was in the past. But in matters that pertain to intellectual and cultural communication and understanding, our investigation has to conclude that the gulf between the old world and the new is still very deep. In fact anti-Americanism in the form of critical hostility toward American thought and culture has been increasing sharply. In recent years it has been steadily promoted also by Soviet cultural diplomacy, which has given highest priority to Western Europe since 1951.

## CONCLUSIONS

In the introduction to this chapter, we argued that the most realistic and effective interchange among cultures and among artists would proceed without reference to foreign policy, and that even if public funds were used to assist such interchange this principle, ideally, should still prevail. But if broad political principles were needed to justify any activities by the United States government in these areas, it was said, then they should be kept broad and be at least generally related to the most basic philosophical assumptions underlying Western society, such as its ideal of man as an individual with paramount rights. It was doubted that the arts could, without risk to their own peculiar values, be employed for temporary and shifting objectives of national interest, such as increasing popular understanding of United States policies and institutions in particular regions of the world.

A corollary assumption is that art and cultural activities generally have a true importance for relatively small minorities in any society, even though these minorities contain those who cultivate and influence intellectual opinions and currents, and who thus have an importance beyond their numbers.

Our first two conclusions derive from this context: cultural exchange activities should not be confused with short-range "information" programs; and both legislative and administrative arrangements for government support of inter-cultural movements should permit longer range planning. The implementation of these two conclusions would be greatly facilitated by acceptance of the third; the centralization of cultural affairs activities of the government in one office in Washington, and giving the cultural affairs officer abroad a status equal to that of the public affairs officer, through whom he now works in the normal USIS arrangement. In 1967 the morale of the cultural affairs officers was so impaired as to create a major problem for an objectives in U.S. cultural activities abroad.

It is beyond the scope of this chapter to attempt to weigh all the arguments in Washington and in the field about the coordination and centralization of cultural activities being carried out by the State Department, USIA, AID, and other agencies. And yet it does appear that the role of cultural exchange within the present complex of USIA activities is a good deal more "muddy" and confused today than it was. As a new and insecure Agency with ill-defined objectives, status and relationship to the Department of State and other government branches including the White House, USIA leadership seems to have tried to protect its role—essential indeed—by attempting constantly to be in the vanguard of the shifting spotlight on day-to-day crises in foreign policy. Such flexibility and alertness is no doubt appropriate to the fast media of which USIA disposes—although there is a question whether even the fast media should be primarily responsive to very short-range issues.

But what seems beyond question is that a preoccupation with the immediate has no place in a serious cultural program. We would further say that the present hierarchy of values within USIA should be reversed, and the higher priority in planning, staffing and financing should go to the long-range cultural program. If such a prospect is altogether utopian and at variance with the present order of values in American society itself, then one has to conclude reluctantly that cultural activities should be administratively severed from USIA information activities, and placed either within the Department of State (where AID and the Peace Corps now are), or in a new independent office combining all the cultural programs now variously handled by USIA, the State Department, AID and others. In such an event, to be sure, USIA officers now serving in an information or public affairs capacity should have the opportunity to transfer without loss of rank to the cultural program, if their preparation and interest so qualify them.

In introducing this chapter, we said that the farther one

moves from an ideal situation in which intercultural movements spontaneously manifest the vitality and the needs of
the artists themselves, the more one needs to cling to strictly
artistic considerations when he attempts to use the arts for
other large purposes. We also argued the importance of
ensuring for such activities the moral and intellectual support of the artistic community at home and abroad. Our
fourth conclusion, therefore, is that no program of international cultural exchange, and no administrative system
for executing it, can succeed without profiting at every turn
from the intensive and realistic advice of artists and artistic
directors themselves. This would seem to be obvious, but
even so it has too often escaped the grasp of the State
Department and USIA in Washington.

Prior to 1963, neither the composition nor the use made
of the Advisory Committee on the Arts reflected artistic
considerations or even an awareness of their importance. A
small Music Advisory Panel in the USIA was better used.
Social, jurisdictional, even "log-rolling" vagaries characterized the employment of the American National Theatre and
Academy as the operating instrument for the President's
Cultural Presentations Program in the State Department.
But worst of all was the feeling among Washington officials responsible for cultural exchange that artists and
artistic directors are by nature difficult, impractical,
or mysterious in the role of consultants. Few government
officials ever tried to learn what the arts and the artists are
about.

Anyone who has had experience in developing programs
through the exclusive employment of artists and artistic
directors as consultants, realizes that the government's
greatest weakness in its intercultural activities has been the
absence of practical, moral, and intellectual support by
those persons who understand artistic enterprises. It is also
a tribute to the shortsightedness of congressional committees and certain top government officials that the manner
in which the government entered the arts on the international scene *a priori* convinced a majority of professionals
in the arts that the United States should stay out of the
field at home.

After the December, 1962, report by Roy Larsen, Chairman of the Advisory Committee on the Arts, and Glenn G. Wolfe of the State Department, Assistant Secretary of State for Educational and Cultural Affairs Lucius Battle dropped ANTA as the housekeeping authority for the cultural presentations program, and ostensibly gave the Advisory Committee on the Arts greater responsibility. The members, appointed for three years and all distinguished in the arts, are asked to develop broad categories and policies. The four advisory panels nominate particular artists or groups. There is no doubt that the State Department post officers abroad, and even indirectly the Congress, have since 1962 been forced by the Advisory Committee to pay more attention to professional and artistic issues. Larsen and his group have formed a counter force of real value to the whole program. But only a general hope that time might be on its side has kept the committee together. Congress, the transitory problems of each post, and other bureaucratic or political pressures still appear to outweigh professional standards, and the sharp reduction in an already inadequate budget for the whole program has been another source of discouragement. The many shifts in State's Educational and Cultural Affairs office are also taken as evidence that neither the administration nor Congress has much interest in the whole effort.

Reorganization and reorientation of the government's administration of cultural exchange are also involved in our fifth conclusion: governments, even more than private foundations, must act with extreme care when trying to use non-American local organizations for cultural activities that professedly are related to American foreign policy. In the mid-fifties, officials in Washington, by agreeing to strong decentralization of authority to public affairs officers in the field, in effect let their own proper control go by default. At times important amounts of local operating currencies of USIA have been tied up in recurring grants to activities managed by others than Americans and sometimes actually anti-American in propaganda, either consciously and subtly or through sheer ignorance about United States policies.

Our broadest conclusion, of course, must go to the question of the worth, actual and potential, of United States international cultural activities. It is clear from the text that in the opinion of the authors, we should have to judge these activities not to have been an important category of United States expenditures if we used only the yardstick of a "better image" of America abroad. It is clear, however, that we are not in sympathy with judging international exchange from the point of view either of competition with the Soviets or of short-term improvements in foreign understanding of American policies. In our opinion, the reduction of our activities in Europe to the advantage of activities elsewhere was not based upon assumptions that were valid *either* for intercultural objectives or for foreign policy considerations. Our final conclusion is that our international cultural activities should be expanded.

We all need to explore three myths that have been taken for granted since about 1948—the myth about European colonialism, the myth about European understanding of Americans through an historical sharing of common values, and the myth that "information" programs can be trusted to relate Americans and Europeans toward common values.

The myth about colonialism has led to the theory that we should disassociate ourselves as much as possible from the European colonial powers and deal only directly with the new and emerging nations. But now we are beginning to see that the new nations, once they are free, are still in need of Europe and in fact wish to import many of their ideas and values from her, including their evaluation of United States culture. For this and other reasons, we have to work with Europe now, facing the problems not only of an Atlantic community but of relating this community to the underdeveloped parts of the world. Furthermore, rightly or wrongly, the European governments, for example the French, argue that Vietnam proves the United States and not themselves to bear the worst stigmas of colonialism.

That the Europeans automatically share our values and understand us is a myth that has been exploded. Some Americans stationed in Europe predicted this development for years, but their long battle to convince us was frustrated both by the complacency of many of their local colleagues and by the desire of administrators and legislators in Washington to hear only about success and novelty.

Related to this former complacency about the solidarity

of the Atlantic Community is the naive idea it can be kept up to date by international programs that concentrate on "news" and "information." It may be necessary, in order to change the mentality, to abandon the name "United States *Information* Agency," even if the recommendations made above for taking cultural activities out of the USIA should become necessary and be adopted.

If the arts and the humanities are of any use at all to the government's objectives, they are of use only to those of the longest range and concerned with the most basic intellectual and cultural currents running among peoples of varying political and economic origins. The assumptions that underlie the international objectives we share with Western Europe have to do with the values people live by. And here the arts and the humanities, if not distorted from their own realities, have a role to play.

# 3. Education, Foreign Policy, and International Relations

## C. EASTON ROTHWELL

Education has become a central and urgent concern in every nation of the world. It has become a dominant element in their domestic policies. It shares with national security and economic interchange a principal role in their foreign policies. In consequence, education has become a major ingredient in the process of international relations.

The phenomenon of concern about education is not new; rather, it has acquired new dimensions and a new intensity in the swift, universal change that characterizes the closing years of the twentieth century. At every critical period in human history, when old institutions and ideas were losing their hold under the impact of new and often revolutionary forces, education has been elevated to a heightened role as both catalyst and interpreter of change. It has been integrally related to all basic changes and has served as one means towards their implementation. This was true as the Hellenic greatness of Greece gave way under the conquests of Alexander and other forces to the more universal and more confused Hellenistic era. It was true as the medieval period crumbled with the rise of nations and of capitalism, the great explorations and discoveries, the Renaissance and the Protestant Revolution. It was especially true as developing science and rationalism brought about the Enlightenment of the 17th and 18th centuries, the cradling period of our contemporary civilization. And it was true as Japan, after centuries under the Shogunate, achieved the matrix of modernity through the Meiji reformation a century ago.

Education plays the same role today in magnified scope

and on universal scale as all humankind moves across another great watershed in its history. We have been brought to the present watershed in part by epoch-marking scientific and technological advances: by the menace and promise of nuclear fission, by the breaking of space barriers, by the extension and quickening of the thinking process through the computer, by the wholesale conquest of disease, by the revolution in communications that has reduced the globe to a small place, free of remoteness and teeming with swift interaction. With facilitation from technology and from the unfortunate but powerful catalyst, war, there have been human changes, also of revolutionary dimension. There has been an almost unmanageable increase in human knowledge, now doubling virtually every decade. Culture has been universalized, even as national consciousness has mounted. It has been universalized at the sidewalk level of the cola stand, the juke box, the bicycle or Honda, the cinema. And it has been universalized at the sophisticated levels of artistic creation, intellectual intercourse, and probing industrial and commercial venture. At these elevated levels, it has been served by private and public associations of artists, intellectuals, educators and businessmen, by professional journals and other media of communication, and by research institutes, all of international scope and perspective.

Another force that has brought us to the late twentieth century watershed, and a powerful one, is the final passing of colonial empires and the consequent emergence of some sixty new nations. This transformation, also of epochal significance, originated in our century, was accelerated by the Second World War and is still in progress. Except in Korea, Vietnam, and, in lesser measure, North Africa, India and Pakistan, it has been achieved with comparatively little bloodshed. From the standpoint of potential difficulty, however, the crisis has not yet passed. The new nations, crowding into the United Nations, have not only changed the composition of that organization, but also the political and economic configurations of the world. Moreover, like the other changes that are ushering us into a new era, the birth of these nations and the high aspirations of their peoples, confronts us with fresh and difficult problems.

## EDUCATION IN THE PRESENT ERA

As we move into that period and meet its problems, education once more serves as catalyst, interpreter, and means of implementation. But now it must do more. It must be the means toward forecast and planning, and it must provide the wisdom and perspective that will serve as a regulator of change, in the very best sense of that term. So great is the need for learning that is is not extreme to state that the world is in the midst of an educational crisis.

Though the forces that have brought us into crisis, the same forces that have brought us to the crest of our watershed, are many and diverse, they pose in educational need two principal centers of focus. The first of these is the urgent need to prepare young minds that can cope wisely, responsibly, and courageously with the grave problems of attaining both stability and freedom while at the same time achieving peace amidst the tensions and conflicts that will be the growing pains of the new era. The second focus, closely related to the first, is the need to meet the educational challenge posed by the new and developing nations with their hundreds of millions of peoples in whom nationhood has aroused potentially explosive expectations.

## EDUCATION FOR CITIZENSHIP

The first focus, that which pertains to freedom, peace, and general well-being, is of concern to all nations, but in greater measure to those that are modernized and wealthy and wield power. On the assumption, commonly accepted but not always practiced, that government must rest upon and be responsive to a broad citizen base, the first focus is really upon education for intelligent citizenship. It implies a citizenry sufficiently knowledgeable and skilled to appraise and help shape the goals of its nation and to assist through its legislative and administrative agencies in the attainment of those goals. Recognizing how far short of this ideal we of the United States have fallen too frequently, as have the people of other long established democratic nations with broad educational opportunities, the distance the world must travel to achieve everywhere well-educated citizenries appears very long. Yet no one can gainsay the ideal.

The requirements for responsible and wise citizenries have never in history been more acute.

The education of a citizen equipped to help shoulder the responsibilities of his nation in the world is neither simple nor easy, because the responsibilities are complex and difficult. They necessitate in the first place the basic civilizing and liberalizing of the human being who is to function as citizen. He must learn to view life as "an important and even beautiful experience for every man," to see it as "something precious, not to be taken or given lightly." As his learning draws upon the human heritage, he must acquire the discipline of reason, a sense of the nobility of man's highest achievements, a taste of the satisfaction of self-fulfillment, a profound regard for the high potential of his fellow humans, and respect for the conditions of freedom and opportunity that will help them attain that potential. Upon this foundation, the citizen must build a sure knowledge of his own society and of the manner in which it works, so that he may exert himself within it. Be he farmer, or artist, leader of industry or craftsman, technician or professional, if he is to function as citizen he cannot avoid learning as the citizen of Athens learned, the process and mechanisms of his own political environment. For only in this manner can he help shape the goals of his nation and exercise his citizen's judgment on the methods of their attainment. Specifically, he must understand how policies are made and decisions taken by those to whom he has entrusted these powers, and how in turn he can make his voice heard in this process. Beyond this, he must learn the qualities to seek in the leadership he chooses, not least, the kinds of education and experience he should insist upon in this elite. In some countries, unfortunately, he must also learn how to establish this kind of political environment.

If the citizen is to perform his international role, he must understand certain basic things about the world. He must know the peoples and nations that constitute the world and the place of his own country within this complex. He must gain insight into the relationships that tie these nations and peoples together and make them dependent upon one another. One of his more difficult tasks will be to understand the differences in culture that cause other peoples to respond to international situations in ways he cannot readily comprehend. Even more difficult may be the development of his appreciation of the principle of cultural diversity as a valuable and creative force in the world.

These are heavy demands, and they will too often go unmet, even in the most advanced countries. They nevertheless stand as goals at which to aim as educational statesmanship lays its strategy to cope with the world crisis in learning.

## EDUCATION FOR DEVELOPMENT

Urgency is more apparent in the second focus of educational need, that of helping the new nations fulfill the great expectations with which they have emerged from the ashes of the colonial period. This need is fourfold. Ways must be found to close more rapidly the gap between the aspirations for education of the newly independent nations and their capabilities for providing it, in terms of both human and material resources. Steps must be taken to meet a more aggravating problem, the differential in educational opportunity between the advanced nations and the developing ones. Not only the pride of young nations and the hunger of their peoples for education make this problem acute. Both the people and their leaders look to the school and the university as instruments for an assault upon not only ignorance, but also poverty, disease, inequality, and other forms of insufficiency. And finally, the timetable of education development must be speeded up to offset the understandable impatience of young nations not only for the conquest of insufficiencies, but perhaps more importantly, for modernization. These nations, some of them new only in the sense of having a recently gained greater measure of independence, have before them as models the modernization of Japan in a century, that of the Soviet Union in half a century, and the partial modernization of certain Latin American nations in even less time. In an age of supersonic travel, communication satellites, rocketry, and instant computerized calculation, or perhaps more importantly of small planes that interlace their own air space over roadless jungles, the new nations can be forgiven their impatience. Their leadership knows, as the world should know, that high expectations unmet can sour into disillusionment and thus become another element of tension in areas already afflicted with tension.

## What Is Now Being Done?

What then is being done to meet the educational crisis at its two principal centers of focus? The brief and simple answer is that very much is being done, but that much more is needed. Present efforts must at the least be doubled, present expenditures greatly increased.

As Rene Maheu, Director-General of the United Nations Educational, Scientific and Cultural Organization (UNESCO) informed world educators gathered at the 1966 Williamsburg Conference on the educational crisis, education, far from languishing, is booming. "It has never before commanded such extensive means and resources, never received so much attention and thought from the public authorities, the citizens at large, specialists and members of the teaching profession." Yet the world's schools, colleges, and universities are far from meeting the demands placed upon them in this critical period of growth.

Everywhere there have been in recent years rapid increases in enrollment in elementary schools, secondary schools, and colleges and universities. The world school and college population grew almost one fourth between 1957 and 1961, from 363 million to 447 million. As might be expected, the comparative rates of growth varied according to urgent need. Growth in the nations of Africa, Asia, and some portions of the Americas, as well as in the Soviet Union, was at least twice as great as that in the countries of Europe. Moreover, the rate of enrollment growth surged well ahead of population growth. In the world as a whole the number of students enrolled grew about twice as fast as the population; in Asia and Africa it grew three times as fast. Everywhere except in the Soviet Union, the number of students attending increased faster in the universities than in the secondary or elementary schools. In Asia, university enrollments grew over 50 percent more than those at the lower levels, as emerging nations made heroic efforts to provide professional skills for their development and raise the educational levels of their people. At the same time, there was a strengthening of secondary education, particularly in those nations that had already begun to provide free and compulsory elementary education.

The financial support of education has increased even more spectacularly than enrollments. During the past fifteen years, public expenditure has risen by an average of 6.5 percent in the industrialized countries and 12.5 percent in the developing countries, according to UNESCO data. The rate of increase has been, in most cases, "higher than that of the budget and much higher than that of national income."

These comparative figures, encouraging as they are, may mislead if one overlooks the basic fact that the developing countries have had much farther to go than the industrialized countries. Three sets of figures will make this vividly clear. One third of the children of school age in the world, almost all of them in the developing countries, still have no school to attend, and there are still 700 million illiterate adults in the world. Whereas the average enrollment in higher education grew by three times in the United States between 1930–34 and 1955–59, from about one million to three, that in Africa increased six times in the same period from about 22 thousand to 133 thousand, while that of all Asia expanded almost seven times from just over 300 thousand to about 2.1 million. Or, to put the same comparison in financial terms, in 1950, when public expenditure on education for the whole world amounted to 34 billion dollars, expenditure in the developing countries was no more than one and a half billion, or less than 5 percent of the total. By 1967, again according to UNESCO data, the proportion of expenditure in developing countries had risen to 10 percent of the total, or approximately ten billion out of one hundred billion.

In the light of the first educational concern, the elevation of citizen intelligence and judgment concerning international affairs and the conduct of foreign policy, one must not overlook the importance of what is happening in the industrialized nations. They, too, have experienced substantial growth in enrollment at all levels, school population increasing at least twice as fast as general population. This has resulted from heightened aspirations for education, and its further democratization. Both may be illustrated by the greater demand for higher education, and the consequent founding of new institutions. Undergraduate enrollments in the United States, approximately six million in 1967–68, are expected to grow to about 15 million by the year 2000. One observer points out that "if all existing institutions doubled in size during the last third of the century, even then we would still need about 1,000 new four-year institutions and perhaps as many as 2,000 new junior colleges to handle the projected expansion." Although general school and college enrollments did not grow as rapidly in the United Kingdom as in the United States, the establishment of the university grants system did bring about a great expansion in the facilities for higher education. More universities, fourteen, were founded between 1948 and 1965 than in all Britain's history prior to the Second World War. During the seven centuries before 1948, eleven universities were established, beginning with Oxford and Cambridge. Other European countries have experienced a comparable burgeoning of education, based upon essentially the same motivation. The Soviet Union, which must be viewed as an industrialized nation, has had an increase in university attendance proportionately greater than either the United States or Europe, and its school enrollments have grown even faster.

Meanwhile, insufficiency continues to afflict the developing nations, despite their spectacular advances. The gap between the educational opportunity they are able to provide and that of the industrial nations is great and immediately threatening. The narrowing of this gap at a sufficiently rapid pace to prevent domestic problems within the developing countries will be beyond the local resources of many of these countries, who are already spending on education greater sums than competing needs would warrant. The recent gathering of world educators, confronting this problem, urged that presently untapped funds, private and public, within the developing countries, be used to meet this crisis. Even with this help, the financial need will remain crucial. The educators pointed out that if only ten percent of the 150 billion dollars presently allocated to defense measures in the world's national budgets, could be diverted to education, many of the specific educational needs could be met. They deplored the present disparity in expenditures as a "dismal commentary on the world's priorities." The Director-General of UNESCO was more explicit. "We must all know, in our hearts, that if our generation were obliged to acknowledge, at the bar of history, that it has not had enough money for education . . . because it is spending a large proportion of its resources on the production of means of destruction, powerful enough to endanger the very survival of our species, or at least of our civilization, it would incur a burden of guilt for which there might be no pardon." Mr. Maheu nevertheless directed attention to a more practical and immediate goal. He indicated that at the present rate of growth the educational needs of the developing countries would require an additional two billion dollars between 1967 and 1970. He urged, therefore, that the one billion dollars of aid, both bilateral and international, now flowing annually into education be at least doubled by 1970.

## THE QUALITY OF WHAT IS BEING DONE

To draw conclusions about what problems we face in education solely upon the basis of data concerning mounting enrollments and escalating but inadequate financial support would be fallacious. It is also necessary to reach some qualitative judgments about the kinds of education presently being provided in both the industrialized and the developing countries, and the manner in which present financial support is being used. As preparation for making these inquiries, it is necessary to clear away some of the mythology concerning the effects of education upon human conduct, particularly in the realm of national and international conduct. Too frequently it is assumed that education *per se* in any amount will lead toward peace by reducing tensions and conflict. The cold facts of history, unfortunately, will not support this assumption. In too many instances it has been the better educated leadership rather than the less educated majority that has provoked international tension. In twentieth century revolutions, and in those that preceded the present century, the educated elite has provided the spearhead of leadership and the theoretical and ideological justification for what is sought or accomplished. Education in itself has not proved to be "the world's best defense against the tensions, misunderstanding, and ignorance that lie at the base of much national conflict." It is possible that education might perform this function if it were always capable of producing disciplined and critical minds, and if it carried with it conversion to values in which international harmony were cherished, and if these values were firmly imbedded in commitment and strongly buttressed by moral courage. Unfortunately, this has happened too infrequently.

In one other respect common generalizations about education require challenge. No one who has lived through the past forty years can avoid the conclusion that superficial or insufficient education can be dangerous. Even a university education, if it has failed to develop a capacity to think and to reach considered judgments, can be both unproductive and hazardous. The rise of communism both in Europe and in Asia, and mob manipulation of the Nazi and Fascist movements bear witness to this conclusion, as do some of the irrational movements that have on occasion swept our own nation, causing normally sane and educated men to behave as bigots.

Having stated these skeptical observations about education, or rather about uncritical statements concerning what education can do, one must return to the positive affirmation of its values. The almost instinctive and often touching faith in education which most people of the United States have manifested for a century and a half, and which many other peoples, including the recently independent ones, have also learned to cherish, rests upon something very real. Without education, no people anywhere could have liberated itself from the scourges of poverty and ignorance, nor gained the skills with which to surmount those forces in the world that would limit the growth of the individual and his society. Without education men would have been restricted in their capacities for invention and creation, and doomed to live with little knowledge of the human heritage.

The challenge in any society is to produce a genuinely educated human being, and to be neither misled nor satisfied with the mere forms and appearances of education.

Truly educated men and women will have in common a certain nucleus of knowledge and the capacity and desire to attain more. They will have experience in rendering and sustaining critical and independent judgment, and a discipline of intellect that will enable them to think and act with wisdom. They will have these qualities, and often a capacity for innovation, regardless of the culture and country in which they have been nurtured. With our deepening understanding of the human psyche and our ever greater insight into the ways of learning there is greater hope that our schools and universities can help boys and girls to become well-educated men and women. This must be our goal and the principal criterion by which we judge both the educational system of our own nation and the evolving systems of others.

It is with this yardstick of quality that we must look again at the stark figures of educational growth, as measured by enrollments, support, and the founding of new institutions. Obviously, we shall find great variations in quality as we look at developing education on a world scale. We find variation of sometimes distressing proportions even when we examine the schools of our own cities and countryside. If the range is great in countries that are hurrying to modernize and often seeking, at the same time, to break the shackles of tradition, this should be understandable.

Elementary, secondary, and college or university education is plagued almost everywhere, but particularly in the developing countries, by frequently inadequate facilities and equipment, by an insufficient number of well educated and trained teachers, and by curriculum content and teaching approaches often ill adapted either to the development of a well-educated person or to the specific needs of the country. Even the poorest nation can display some educational institutions of high quality; and even the richest of nations harbors substandard schools, and colleges and universities of sufficiently dubious quality to be regarded as "diploma mills." Everywhere there is wastage, as students leave school, or are required to repeat classes, wastage that reduces the significance of enrollment increases. And almost everywhere there is the tendency to cling to outmoded building and equipment standards, unless there is bold and imaginative leadership to replace them with more modern and functional designs. These are problems in wealthy countries; they are even more acute problems in developing countries which, for example, are now allocating as much as 5 to 15% of the national budget to the building of schools.

What steps need to be taken in education on a world scale to overcome the most serious deficiencies, and to establish norms of planning and practice that will lead toward the guiding criterion, the development of genuinely educated human beings and the meeting of society's most important needs? Fortunately much thought has been given to this question.

### A MODEL FOR DEVELOPMENT

A synthesis of views expressed in recent studies or voiced in recent conferences by educators from several continents, presents a coherent and stimulating model for future growth:

*Illiteracy*—With funds, and with a sufficient number of teachers trained in proved techniques for the development of literacy, an effort can be made to help 700 million illiterate adults learn to read and write. The task must be carried out by individual nations, within their villages and cities, but it will require international assistance, both monetary and human. The elimination of illiteracy can be further hastened by much-needed additional research on methods.

*Elementary education*—The world trend toward free and compulsory education at the elementary level should be extended as rapidly as possible until it is universal. This would help satisfy the prevalent hunger for learning and, at the same time, build the essential foundations for a strong system of secondary and higher education. It is an indispensable step in the radical transition now taking place from the education of elites to mass education. This in turn is integral to the democratization of societies and political structures.

*Secondary Education*—As rapidly as feasible, secondary education should also be made accessible to all boys and girls, both for the reasons that apply to elementary education, and because the development of the nation must depend upon skills cultivated in the secondary schools. The nations must likewise rely upon these schools to provide the candidates for higher education and professional training.

*Higher Education*—Higher education, presently growing more rapidly than either secondary or elementary education, must continue to expand as the scientific, technological and humanistic demands of development continue to increase. The universities need numerous reforms in the content of the education they offer, their approaches to learning, the professional preparation they provide, and their capacities to serve as creative forces within their societies. These needs will be discussed at greater length below.

*Coordinated education*—Within all countries, industrialized as well as developing, education at all levels must be considered as a unified whole and there must be workable articulation between the three principal levels. Only thus will the nation use one of its greatest assets most effectively to meet its requirements, not least among them a well-educated citizenry. Only thus will the intellectual and social mobility become possible that are so essential to a democratic society.

*Good teachers*—The good teachers and professors who are at the heart of good education are in short supply in all nations, industrialized and developing, although the shortage is more acute in the new nations. Better education and training is needed for elementary and secondary teachers, especially in the developing countries, where many who teach today, particularly at the primary level, are inadequately qualified. Fortunately, the reform of teacher preparation is in progress in many developing nations, India being conspicuous among them. Fortunately also, it is taking place within our own nation. Because the need is great to make education a major force in social development, "both the teacher and the classroom must become an integral part of the social process that is transforming their society." This means that the institutions which prepare teachers must be conscious of that social process. They must also be actively involved in research and experiment looking toward the improvement of schools as well as the better preparation of teachers. To attract and hold good teachers, the conditions of their employment and their salaries must be at competitive levels.

*The students*—The schools and colleges must ever be mindful that it is the student who learns, and that teaching is a means to that end. No nation has a monopoly on educational approaches in which this principle is central, nor upon the good teaching it requires. No nation, developed or developing, is without need to reaffirm the principle continuously and to assure that it is put into practice. Everywhere it is essential to draw the student actively into the learning process from the day he begins his schooling, and to sustain that relationship through college and graduate work. Learning then becomes a mutual and creative enterprise involving both the student and the teacher as learners. Experience demonstrates that the students will respond eagerly to this approach. To introduce it, however, will require in many instances, particularly in secondary schools and colleges, overcoming present outlooks and traditional practices.

*Educational programs*—The present content of education in many societies is ill-adapted to their present and changing needs. Curricula are too frequently crowded, over-diversified, and lacking in a sense of wholeness and organic development from year to year. In these respects curricula are inadequately attuned to the needs and development of the maturing student. In the secondary schools, and especially in the universities, there is a tendency to cling to classical education, at a time when preparation for the vocations and professions is not only in the national interest but gives the student greater assurance of employment. In both agricultural and industrial nations, a practical emphasis is indispensable. At the same time, the curriculum planner must bear in mind that the student will be a citizen as well as a workman or professional. His education cannot neglect the intellectual capacities for that role or it will be short-sighted. Nor can it escape the premise, indispensable to genuine democracy, that every individual is entitled to learning opportunities that will cultivate and extend his or her capacities to their fullest capabilities. The reconciliation of these requirements will not be easy, but it will be urgently important.

*Teaching approaches*—In the preceding paragraph on the student, the learning-teaching relationship which is perhaps the most important element in good teaching has been stated. It needs affimation and reaffirmation in countries at all stages of development, particularly in the secondary schools and the universities. Techniques that help good teaching are known, have been tested in experimentation, and placed in practice. Their introduction where they are needed can be accomplished through schools for teacher preparation and by in-service training. Technology to assist teaching—the film, radio, television and programmed instruction, for example—is inadequately known and used. Instruction concerning these tools and their potential is needed in teachers' colleges, as well as in demonstration centers.

*The administering of education*—The skilled and enlightened administration of the educational system of a nation is a vitally important but complicated task. It requires at every level, from the elementary school to the ministry of education, men and women of first quality, preferably drawn from the teaching profession, but equipped by experience and special training to shoulder the responsibilities of a costly and complex enterprise in which the growth of human beings and the meeting of society's requirements must be the dominant motivation. The necessary tools of administration are the trained capacity to plan and to use wisely the resources at hand for the fulfillment of the plan, together with managerial skills such as the responsible handling of funds, the capacity to obtain them from public and private sources, the ability to direct and to lead a staff, and other capabilities familiar to almost every business or profession. More important, of course, is the quality of educational statesmanship that can not only grasp the details of the educational system and perceive them in their whole, but can also foresee new needs, relate them to existing structure and practice, and lead the system wisely toward enlarged and modified goals. Training is available in some countries for school administrators, principally in the colleges or departments of "pedagogy" or "education" within the universities. College and university administrators are normally recruited from among scholars who have had on-the-job administrative preparation. In developing countries the more rapid provision of good administrators at all levels may be facilitiated by the establishment of training centers closely related to institutions in which all other aspects of the educational process are being studied and taught. Administrators and prospective administrators can profit from opportunities to exchange visits within their own countries or to visit other countries and educational systems.

*Evaluation, planning and research*—Continuing analysis and evaluation of the educational system is indispensable, whether in young systems or more mature ones. This requires adequately trained personnel for the gathering of information. In some countries, they may have to be obtained on loan from other nations or trained abroad. There must be adequate arrangements for the evaluation of progress toward the goals of the system, and there must be the trained capacity to adapt to both the goals and practices of evolving needs. Wise evaluation will penetrate bureaucratic obfuscation and discern obstructions where these exist and will be aware of the necessities for flexibility and the capacity for innovation. Periodic scrutiny, "friendly but critical," by sources outside the nation can likewise be important. It can be arranged either on a bilateral basis, through regional organizations, through international bodies such as the International Association of Universities, or through UNESCO. Evaluation is the handmaiden of planning, now a priority need in all educational systems. All appraisal, all planning, and all development will inevitably be reinforced and rendered more intelligent by adequate programs of research on every major aspect of education. Some of the research can be accomplished with private resources or through international assistance in its several forms. In addition, there will be need for public funds. The proposal of Rene Maheu that two percent of the educational budget be devoted to this purpose seems reasonable.

## THE ROLE OF THE UNIVERSITIES

It is a cliche to state that the universities are the capstone of any system of education, but this is nevertheless functionally true. It is demonstrably the universities that provide the greatest proportion of leadership in any society. It is they who constitute the intellectual and creative bridge between adolescence and young adulthood. It is they who prepare men and women professionally for the tasks of development or, in the older countries, the tasks of preservation and growth. It is the universities that have become the principal centers of research on almost all aspects of growth, whether these be scientific and technological, or human. It is the universities also that have become the principal carriers of culture, the locus of research into the folk arts, and of creative innovation in all the visual arts, music, and writing. It is the universities that must carry the burdens of intelligent social and political reform. It is they that must carry the responsibility for helping forward the lower schools, through the education and training of teachers and administrators, through the reform of educational content by the incorporation of new knowledge and new appoaches to knowledge. For these reasons, the role of the universities in the present educational crisis deserves special scrutiny.

There are few nations in the world that do not have a university. Most of these are new and relatively small nations that have recently attained independence. In many of the other new nations, there are good or potentially good universities, testimonials to the colonial heritage from the British, French and Dutch empires. As will be indicated, however, these universities are not always suited to present needs.

The truly great universities of the world can be counted quickly, and are found principally in Europe and North America and in Asia. In these institutions the greatest proportion of the research that goes forward is producing the rapid growth of knowledge. They are providing the professional training, not only for the scholars who carry forward the pure sciences and arts of their disciplines, but also those who will apply knowledge in the conduct of the world's affairs. And they are the principal nucleus of the international community of learning that interlaces the globe, tying together through inter-university arrangements and professional associations men and women of scientific, humanistic and artistic concern. Side by side with the great universities, there stand in many countries, new and old, institutions of lesser stature, ranging all the way down the scale to the diploma mills. Most of the finer universities are principally or heavily supported by their governments. A distinguished minority rely principally upon private funds, although even they receive substantial government assistance in several forms, sometimes in return for research and other functions.

In examining how effectively the universities of the world are meeting the crisis in education, both in terms of the preparation of wisely educated citizens, and in terms of professional and technical assistance to developing nations, one must recognize that there are important differences in the approaches to education between, for example, the traditional British, French, German, Dutch, Spanish systems and the American systems and between any of these and the indigenous systems of certain older Asian countries that have felt the influences of Europe and the United States but have adapted them to local circumstance and need. Each system has its merits and demerits. It would be hazardous to compare them in general terms. Rather, one should ask how well they educate youth at the college or undergraduate level, how well they lead intelligent young men and women toward professional careers in medicine, engineering, law, pedagogy, business, public administration and agriculture. Even the best institutions fall short of ideal performance in all respects. Those which are less than the best fail in greater measure, either because they are not staffed by men and women capable of lifting them to pinnacles of performance, because they are inadequately equipped, because they have lost vitality through the weight of tradition, or because they are too slavishly imitating models inappropriate to the needs of their respective countries.

There is not space within the compass of this essay to examine in detail the relatively small number of universities that have achieved and maintained greatness, and discover how they have done so. It is sufficient to indicate that over decades and centuries they have been able to sustain the motivation that marked their founding and youth. Usually, they have had good fortune in their leadership. Their successive leaders, with only occasional exceptions, have known and preserved the values essential to an institution of higher learning. They have not let structure or mechanics swamp learning and inquiry. Among their leaders and their faculties has been the capacity to understand the university as a whole, and at the same time to perceive and appreciate the necessity for its internal diversity. There has been the ability to adapt the institution to changing times and styles, to whole new ranges of knowledge and technique, without losing sight of those things which must endure.

Consciousness of the responsibility of the university to its society has never, in the best institutions, meant simply a passive acceptance of all that exists within that society. Inquiry and learning are necessarily critical processes. They are also inventive and creative. Within very broad limits of consensus, the best universities have always cherished and protected not only the right to disagree, but also the right to challenge and discuss the existing patterns and values of their social, economic, and political milieu. Universities are therefore often unsettling as well as constructive forces within their societies. The protection of their capacity to perform in this way is at the very heart of academic freedom. In turn, the protection accorded by society obligates the universities to fulfill deeply their social responsibilities.

The role of the university in developing countries is especially complicated and difficult. Of necessity it must be more deeply concerned with the entire system of education, and with the special educational requirements of the nation. If it is attuned to those requirements, the university will bring within its compass professional training in agriculture, engineering, or administration, for example, to meet acute development needs. This may mean a break with the past in which the emphasis has been placed almost wholly on a classical education, with perhaps some attention to law. In some poorer or more sparsely populated countries, post-secondary education not properly at the university level, such as the vocational training of mechanics or agricultural assistants, may also have to find a place in the universities. To sustain it there and at the same time preserve high standards of university performance poses a difficult task.

Vice-Chancellor Kenneth E. Robinson of the University of Hong Kong has pointed out that the carrying out of the essential functions of a university—research, teaching, and public service—may be more difficult in the developing country for several reasons. The increasing demands placed upon them in carrying out each of these functions will have more political implications than elsewhere. Here, the finding of a properly balanced working relationship between university and government will be less easy. Moreover, universities in the developing countries are inevitably engaged in producing a new élite to fill the vacuum created by independence and the requirements of growth. The very existence of this élite can lead to restlessness within the society and may appear to slow the process of democratization. The production of a broadly based, intelligently educated citizenry, so indispensable to stable democratic government, will depend less upon the immediate capabilities of the university than upon the more gradual accretion of education through the elementary and secondary schools, which will in turn offer more qualified candidates for the university. Thus educational mobility will ultimately be increased and the new élite will be more deeply grounded in a democratic base.

Another of the handicaps which the universities must overcome in many developing nations is their continued reliance upon the concepts and methods of the foreign universities which served as models for their establishment during the colonial period. Several observers have noted, for example, a lack of innovation in the Indonesian universities because curricula, organization, and methods of teaching still largely follow the former Dutch pattern. The same story is true in India. The report of the Education Commission 1964–66 of the Government of India stated that "looking at Indian Universities a century after their foundation, one cannot but feel that they have failed to adapt themselves sufficiently to the vast and unique opportunities which surround them. . . . The universities remain alien implantations not integrated into the new India." Unfortunately, the British models were themselves outdated at the time they were being copied in the colonies. The Indian Universities Commission commented in 1950 that it was very unfortunate the Indian Universities founded in the 19th century should have copied the type of the University of London just before that university abandoned the type. And C.E. de Kiewiet, after acknowledging that excellence in building, staffing, and curriculum was a rich and honorable legacy left by the former British rulers in Africa, nevertheless points out that "instead of the most modern university, the British academic world had as by accident exported an anachronism." Their definition of excellence lacked flexibility. They were "invested with attitudes that made them appear far more detached from their environment than the older institutions after which they were modeled." Misunderstandings, misinterpretations and political resentments were born that made later adjustments difficult. "There was lost the invaluable early advantage of defining the role of the university as one bringing it immediately and concretely close to the task of building a new nation. . . . One saw the phenomenon of an institution devoted to tradition, beside a government that could only succeed by breaking with tradition."

Nation building and society developing have become one of the great functions of the university, growing alongside, and requiring integration with its more traditional functions: to discover new knowledge, and to bring about learning. As has been indicated, curriculum must take into account the building blocks of new economies and new nationhood and prepare young men and women for the professions of agriculture, engineering, management, finance and other practical subjects, while at the same time not losing sight of the deep values derivable from a classics curriculum. But they must also put their resources into helping resolve one of the most touchingly human, but potentially explosive, problems of the young developing nation—the movement of great populations from the countryside to the urban slums. With high hope and little knowledge these peoples have made the "unprofitable exchange of rural subsistence for urban poverty, employment for unemployment, or tolerable rural discontent for a dangerous urban frustration." To cope with this problem will require the most understanding cooperation of the government and the university.

## ASSISTANCE FOR EDUCATIONAL DEVELOPMENT

It must be obvious that the mixture of potentially destructive or creative forces at work on the crest of the historic watershed over which the world is now passing find reflection in every facet of education. It must also be clear that even the wealthier countries with well-developed modern educational systems will have difficulty providing enough schools, colleges, and universities of sufficient quality and quantity to meet adequately the problems caused by population growth, the rapid multiplication of knowledge, and the new civic as well as the scientific and humanistic burdens placed upon education. Many of the developing nations will be engaged in bootstrap operations of heroic proportions to meet these urgent and demanding problems of growth. Their resources will be strained and they will need assistance.

Assistance is available in several forms and through a number of different channels. At the world level, the growth of higher education is being assisted by the international professional associations of the several disciplines and professions, such as those in history or chemistry, law or medicine. It is likewise being assisted by the private International Association of Universities, and by such official bodies as UNESCO and the International Bank for Reconstruction and Development, neither of which confines its help, of course, to higher education only. There are also organizations for regional cooperation in Latin America, Asia, and Africa, for example, sometimes with funds to assist in educational improvement, as is true of the Colombo Plan. In addition, there are bilateral arrangements, and limited multilateral ones for either mutual assistance or oneway aid.

It will give concrete dimension to the interlacing and sometimes overlapping patterns of assistance now available to the developing nations to select a single nation for illustration. Let us arbitrarily choose Thailand, partly because it is a country in which there has been a steady increase of assistance, partly because it is the headquarters for a number of regional organizations that influence education, and also because substantial and reliable data concerning Thailand and other Southeast Asian countries has been provided recently by an extensive study conducted jointly by UNESCO and the International Association of Universities.

Educational improvement in Thailand has been of concern to several international bodies: the United Nations proper through its technical assistance program and the United Nations Special Fund; several of the specialized agencies, including the International Bank, the World Health Organization, the International Labor Organization, in addition to the specially created International Development Association, and, of course, UNESCO, which actually maintains in Bangkok its Regional Office for Education in Asia.

At the same time, Thailand receives regional support and assistance from a number of organizations, some of them cooperative ventures it has helped to found. For example, Thai education benefits from three Institutes, all established by Asian states with assistance from UNESCO: that on Educational Planning and Administration at New Delhi, that on the Training of Teacher Educators at Quezon City in the Philippines, and that on School Building Research, with headquarters at Bandung, Indonesia. In addition, it derives assistance from the Southeast Asia Science Cooperation Center in Djakarta in the development of scientific and technological research. Moreover, Thailand participated in conferences of the Ministers of Education of Asian Member States, the third of which, jointly sponsored in 1965 by ECAFE and UNESCO, looked toward an overall plan for Asian education at all levels, with projections to 1980.

Thus far, we have been concerned with regional bodies growing from joint efforts with international organizations. Thailand is involved, however, in others of more strictly regional scope. For example, it has participated in the activities of SEATO under its Cultural Relations Program. Attention has been given to the problems of equivalence among the educational systems within the region and to the language problems of Southeast Asia. A SEATO Commission on Equivalence has actually set out to reduce by unilateral, bilateral, or multilateral action the barriers to movement from one institution to another in Southeast Asia. As evidence of more tangible help, 132 Thai graduate students were accepted at the SEATO Graduate School of Engineering between 1959 and 1964.

There are still other indigenous organizations of a regional character, of which Thailand is a member. In 1956

Chulalongkorn University of Thailand participated with representatives of a number of other distinguished institutions in Southeast Asia in the establishment of the Association of Southeast Asian Institutions of Higher Learning. This Association, with headquarters in Bangkok, planned seminars in 1965 on "The Role of Universities in Social and Economic Development in Southeast Asia," on "Agriculture and Veterinary Science," on "The Role of Universities in Human Resource Development," and on "Engineering and Technological Studies." For 1966 the association planned follow-up seminars on Mathematics, Sociological Jurisprudence, and the Teaching of Philosophy, together with new seminars on Language Problems in Southeast Asian Universities, and the Role of Universities in Southeast Asian Society. Meanwhile, still another organization was evolved to tie together education in Southeast Asia, the Southeast Asian Ministers of Education Council. The secretariat of this organization is also in Bangkok.

Many wealthier nations contribute to all this work of educational development through the international and regional bodies referred to in the previous paragraphs. Some nations, including the United States, maintain, in addition, bilateral programs. Help for the education of Thailand, either monetary or by means of skilled personnel, comes from AID, The Ford Foundation, the Rockefeller Foundation, and the Asia Foundation, among others, together with exchange programs for teachers and students, and the Peace Corps.

It cannot be claimed by any means that the above listing is complete, but even incomplete it must convey the impression that Thailand is scarcely neglected so far as the development of its educational system is concerned. It must also be obvious that Thailand is not passively waiting for help to come, but is actively joining its neighbors, with and without international assistance, to bring about educational advance. In fact, one of the more striking conclusions that may be drawn from this record, is that the developing countries, as represented by Thailand, are, on their own initiative, making intelligent strides towards converting tradition-laden educational systems into instrumentalities for meeting the hard requirements of modernization.

One must not be misled, however, by the mere listing of what is being done in a country such as Thailand, whether through cooperative arrangements, by international or regional agencies, or by individual countries on a bilateral basis. The total effort, as recorded here, seems greater and more sufficient than in fact it is. Even so, Thailand is better off than some of the recently independent African nations, and more favored than some of her own Asian neighbors. These nations do not always have foundations on which to build comparable to those of Thailand, nor are they favorably situated at a regional crossroads.

The average number of students among every 100,000 of Thailand's inhabitants has risen from seven in the period between 1930 and 1934 to 207 in the period between 1955 and 1959. This proportion compares favorably with that of the United Kingdom, but it is about one fifth that of the Soviet Union and less than an eighth that of the United States. A significant portion of Thailand's gross national product goes to support education, and she has one of the more distinguished universities of Asia. Even so, her need is great, not only for education but for all the advantages of modernization that will enable her to hold her own in a modernized world. And although the interlacing network of agencies at work in Thailand, reinforcing her own efforts to improve the quality and capacities of her educational system, have hastened progress remarkably by Asian standards, the pace is still too slow to meet the urgent demands of the great changes which are transforming the world.

## THE ROLE OF INTERNATIONAL AGENCIES

To have singled out one country for purposes of illustration has a further disadvantage. When this procedure is used, one does not always perceive in world dimensions the activities and influences of international organizations, both private and public that are assisting the development of education. It will be sufficient to illustrate this point with some aspects of the work of two organizations, UNESCO, a specialized agency of the United Nations, and the private International Association of Universities.

UNESCO came into being at about the same time as the United Nations, just at the end of the Second World War. It was intended to advance education, science, and culture through international activities. Like other organizations, national and international, concerned with learning and culture, UNESCO did not, in the beginning, obtain the attention it deserved from the major nations whose primary concern was with security, economic rehabilitation, and the practical problems of society and health. The organization nevertheless proceeded in these years to lay the foundations for considerable cultural exchange, and for many educational developments. In a sense, UNESCO found its most promising milieu in the developing nations, as the vestiges of the colonial period crumbled soon after the war. Almost twenty years of work among the new-born nations were crowned by a series of ministerial conferences in the mid-1960's. They were held in Africa in 1964, Asia in 1965, the Arab States in 1966 and Latin America in 1966. The countries involved agreed to raise primary, secondary, and higher education enrollments, while at the same time reducing illiteracy among the 700 million people over fifteen years of age unable to read and write.

The targets of enrollment increase set by these conferences for the period 1965 to 1970 were: elementary education, from 160 to 212 million; secondary education, from 22 to 40 million; and, higher education, from 0.9 to 4 million. Some who have labored at education in the developing countries believe that these goals are unattainable in the period specified, given the conditions in a number of the countries concerned. When norms have been set, however, even though they are beyond immediate reach, if used wisely they can inspire people to attain them. They may even be means of reaching the peoples of other nations who can contribute to educational development.

The International Association of Universities was founded at Nice in 1950, during a Universities Conference attended by 168 universities from 52 countries. Its purpose has been to provide "a center of cooperation at the international level among the universities and similar institutions of higher education of all countries, as well as among organizations in the field of higher education generally." Sixteen years later, the association had 480 university members and had staked out six primary fields of study: (1) the training and recruitment of academic staff; (2) the problem of equivalences of degrees and diplomas; (3) the responsibility of the university towards primary and secondary education; (4) university libraries; (5) systems of university administration; and, (6) the strengthening of international university cooperation and the elimination of obstacles to such cooperation.

The Association could report a substantial body of completed research on a wide range of subjects affecting the improvement of higher education, some of them in cooperation with other international bodies. Its Secretariat stated, however, that there were obstacles to international cooperation among universities over which the universities themselves seemed to have little control. These included "Political conflicts, of whatever degree of violence, for example; and the persistent, even increasing, inequality of economic development in the world—which must unceasingly be denounced as the scandal that it is." The Secretariat continued, "The lack of material resources condemns many university people in developing countries to isolation, and cuts them off from that constant flow of informative exchange which is now indispensable for the progress of research and, consequently, of teaching. Universities in more fortunate countries can only slowly help to remedy this state of affairs."

Commenting upon the dictum of the UNESCO preamble that "wars are born in the minds of men," the Secretariat stated its agreement with this principle in somewhat more restrained form, but went on to say that it implies that wars and conflicts "are partly born, and can therefore be partly avoided, through the work of universities." They added, "Individual universities have each some sense of this great responsibility, but any general commitment to it is yet to be achieved." The statement concluded, however, with a vigorous assertion of the time-honored functions of the university. "The fact is that universities are inevitably the arenas of intellectual conflict, and it would be absurd to expect them to begin preaching some kind of universally benevolent syncretism."

## THE NATURE OF THE UNITED STATES ROLE

We have now reached the point at which it is possible to ask, in sufficient context, what the United States has done and what it should do to assist the growth of education abroad. In addition, one must ask what steps have been taken and should be taken by this nation to adapt its own educational system to current international requirements.

Two kinds of assistance are still required by the developing nations because some have advanced more than others on the road toward modernization. Very substantial assistance to education at all levels is needed in some of the younger, more recently independent, and poorer nations, of which certain young African states are examples. In other countries, which have benefitted more from the colonial educational heritage, and some of which have rich ancient cultures of their own, the greater need may be for new concepts of education, and for professionals skilled in the practical arts and sciences of modernized societies. India is probably a good example of this category.

As we review briefly what the United States had done to meet these needs, it is useful to remember that the strengthening of education among peoples whom we now describe as "developing" has gone forward through missionary endeavor for over a century, and American foundations have given assistance for decades. The great outpouring of official and unofficial aid to education, however, postdates the Second World War, and coincides with two other major developments of great consequence. These were the final stages of the passing of colonialism, on the one hand, and the simultaneous birth and intensification of the Cold War on the other. In actual fact, as well as in Lenin's theories of imperialism, the passing of colonialism and the Cold War were related. While the breakdown of colonialism was hastened by the suicidal wars among the old imperial powers, in Lenin's view, the role of the communist nation was not only to abet this process, but to extend the communist revolution to the emancipated peoples. The effort to carry out this strategy or to counter it became part of the Cold War, a political and ideological battle for predominance wherever the opportunity afforded itself, but particularly in areas of strategic significance.

The great American effort at assistance during the past twenty years was inspired certainly in its initial stages by the Cold War, but was also inspired by the humanitarian

and practical recognition that poverty, ill-health and ignorance could be enemies of peace and stability. This mixture
of motives lay behind the launching of the Point IV program
in 1948. At that moment the educational institutions of this
nation were, for the most part, without experience in sending technical assistance abroad, whether in education or
other fields of development. They lacked in general the understanding of other cultures which business and commercial enterprise had gained in prior years. And they had yet
to learn the imperatives of development, not least among
these the need to fill politically dangerous vacuums left by
the departure of colonial authority. More important perhaps was the equally compelling force of newly aroused
aspirations and expectations.

Twenty years and 100 billion dollars later, as one observer measures the timetable of United States assistance,
the American approach to helping other countries, in education as in other matters, is more sophisticated and professional. It could also be described as sadder and wiser.
We now know that not all aid, even in education, begets
friendship or favor, and that it does not necessarily assure
alignment with the nations and forces that oppose the Soviet
Union or mainland China in the war for allegiances. Moreover, we have learned anew the unhappy circumstance that
literacy gives no patent assurance of stability, and that education, even to the highest level, affords no guarantee of
peace.

The situation is even more sobering. The United States
contribution to assistance, public and private, has been
truly massive since 1948. Its very massiveness has exerted
strong influence on all other sources of assistance to the
developing two-thirds of the world, whether those sources
be international or regional, private or public, or whether
the assistance comes from individual countries, singly or in
small clusters, communist or non-communist.

Despite these facts, we have been losing ground. We have
been losing ground at home rather in the relative size of the
contribution we make to assistance than in public concern
among knowledgable groups. Whereas the appropriations
for aid were 12 percent of the federal budget in 1950, they
were only 2 percent in 1967. In dollar terms, the average of

5 billion dollars annually devoted to assistance from all sources over a twenty year period was reduced in 1967 to between two and a half and three billion. Although four nations at least had apparently passed the point of needing assistance, in general, the economic gap between the developed and the developing nations has actually widened in recent years. This circumstance, together with irritating dissatisfactions in some developing countries such as their objection to what they regard as intervention in their domestic affairs, have made more uneasy in some nations the donor-recipient relationship. On the other hand, many of the undeveloped countries have made real progress. As one observer puts it, "To anyone who has worked in these countries during the past decade . . . there is undeniably a change in the climate of development, a perceivable connection with the future, better-trained people, purposeful institutions, physical infrastructure, that were not there ten years ago." He goes on to state, "there also remain massive and enduring problems in all these areas, plus increasingly evident problems in population growth, urbanization, political maturity, and systems of communication essential to nationhood and international cooperation."

All this, of course, bears upon education. The emerging needs, together with the enduring ones, not only lend justification to the concept of an international crisis in education, but make necessary a reassessment of what our own nation is doing through both public and private sources to meet the urgencies of that crisis.

## THE INTERNATIONAL EDUCATION ACT OF 1966

Until recently, the federal contribution to education in developing countries was buried in the general category of technical assistance and given insufficient visibility. The actual implementation of assistance was frequently made the responsibility of one of our universities. Frictions between the universities and the federal agency, AID, marred the relationship and attenuated the work in the field. Fortunately, both situations were ameliorated. Following a study of the relationships between AID and the universities requested by the administrator of that agency and conducted by John W. Gardner, then president of the Carnegie Corporation of New York, some of the aggravations that made difficult federal assistance through universities to developing nations were identified, and in some measure removed. A very important development, which not only made assistance to education visible, but elevated it to a symbol of the intention of the United States to give world dimensions to the concept of a Great Society, was the enactment of the International Education Act of 1966.

The prelude to the International Education Act was an address given by President Johnson at the Smithsonian Institution in September 1965 in which he proposed "a new and noble adventure." Five months later, in February, 1966, the President in a Special Message to the Congress, outlined a broad program of education bearing upon international affairs and sought legislation to bring the program into being. In doing so, he stated: "Education lies at the heart of our International relations." A substantial portion of the President's proposed program was incorporated into the International Education Act of 1966, which drew wide support from both Houses of Congress. Symbolically, the President signed the bill into law on a visit to Chulalongkorn University in Thailand in October of that year.

Regrettably, funds were not appropriated by the Congress in the following year to implement the Act, in part because of the financial demands of the war in Vietnam. This meant a temporary setback which may have dimmed somewhat the hopes of American educational institutions, who responded to the act with great enthusiasm, and may also have produced negative repercussions abroad. The Act is in being, however, and the President's program is in being and international education will in due time profit from both.

Developing countries stand to profit directly and indirectly from both the Act and the President's program. The President called for enlarged AID assistance to education. Although this probably will not come about until the Vietnam situation is resolved, it is a clear indication of purpose and a guide for policy. Additional assistance would make easier both the exchange of students, and study by potential leaders in the United States. At the student and teacher level, school-to-school partnership will be encouraged. By 1967, 160 such partnerships had been established in 29 countries, with many other applications awaiting implementation. At the same time, plans were worked out for an Exchange Peace Corps, which would bring to the United States young foreigners to serve as teachers and teacher's aides.

The main thrust of the International Education Act, however, was to strengthen international studies in the United States at both the graduate and undergraduate levels. Behind this intent was a two-fold purpose, which can be glimpsed in the preamble to the act:

> The Congress hereby finds and declares that a knowledge of other countries is of utmost importance in promoting mutual understanding and cooperation between nations; that strong American educational resources are a necessary base for strengthening our relations with other countries; that this and future generations of Americans should be assured ample opportunity to develop to the fullest extent possible the intellectual capacities in all areas of knowledge to other countries, peoples, and cultures. . . .

To these ends, the Act would provide grants to graduate centers in American universities as national resources for research and training in "international studies and the international aspects of professional and other fields of studies." It would also draw upon the resources of professional and scholarly associations by means of grants. The overriding purpose of these proposals was to equip this nation to handle with professional skill, both at home and abroad, the relationships and development essential to the conquest of poverty, disease, ignorance and the newer problems of developing countries.

The strengthening of undergraduate programs in international studies has the dual purpose of providing well-equipped and motivated candidates for the graduate programs; but even more of creating an intelligent citizenry with some depth of knowledge about other cultures and countries, and a sufficient understanding of the political process, national and international, to perform with wisdom their citizens' role in the determination and execution of foreign policies.

The need for improved undergraduate education in the

international field was made compellingly evident in a
survey conducted by the Department of Health, Education,
and Welfare. It revealed that no more than half of the
colleges and universities surveyed in 1966 reported offering
a single course in non-Western studies, and that fewer than
two dozen of our 1,500 universities or four-year colleges
seem to require all candidates for the baccalaureate to take
even a single course dealing primarily with non-Western
areas. Fewer than one tenth of the students in four-year
colleges took such courses even when they were offered,
and less than one percent studied a non-Western language.
This deficiency in intellectual horizons and understanding
has special significance when so many of the world's problems in the decades ahead will bear upon the non-Western
regions, and when American concerns, not only those of
scholarship or assistance, but also those of business and
trade will focus with rapid increase of intensity upon these
regions.

This is by no means a comprehensive review of the International Education Act and the President's Program,
both of which constitute notable gains in the effort to bring
about an effective and mature American understanding of
the world, and a much more professional approach to the
growing pains, not only of young nations, but of a world
that is taking its first steps in a new environment born of
technological change and rapid history. Just one other aspect of the International Education Act need be mentioned.
It mobilizes on behalf of international education not only
the universities and colleges, private and public, and the
non-profit associations, public and private, concerned with
education, but also all federal departments and agencies
with functions relevant to education and international development.

## THE ROLE OF THE FOUNDATIONS

The private foundations of the United States have a distinguished record of selective assistance to international
education, both in foreign countries and in this nation. It
would be difficult to arrive at a dollar total of the assistance
they have given, but an examination of the record reveals
no slackening of pace in recent years, and some increase

in the number and variety of projects they have supported. The range of their activities becomes apparent through a few illustrations. Their assistance has reached to virtually every part of the world. Some is of long standing, such as the grants of the Rockefeller Foundation to support developments in health and medicine. Much dates from the conclusion of the Second World War and the passing of the colonial period. Important help has been given by both the Rockefeller and Ford Foundations to improve agriculture in India, for example, and by The Ford Foundation to help adapt village economies to these advances. A substantial grant was made by The Ford Foundation to the Catholic University of Valparaiso, Chile, to develop a School of Business, and another to the new Chinese University of Hong Kong to develop research and a graduate program, and for data-processing equipment. The Danforth Foundation meanwhile gave a substantial sum to Operation Crossroads Africa, to a summer workcamp program in Africa for American students, while The Ford Foundation granted funds to the Niels Bohr Institute of Denmark to exchange physicists with Eastern Europe, China, India, Brazil and other countries.

These are but a few examples of a large scale and diversified philanthropic enterprise that is shared by dozens of foundations, large and small. Under the broad rubric of "international activities," these organizations have assisted the fields of cultural relations, education, the exchange of persons, health and medicine, international studies at centers in the United States and abroad, peace and international cooperation, relief and refugees, and technical assistance. Twice each year a compilation of grants in these fields and others is issued by The Foundation Library Center, situated in New York. It is an enlightening and encouraging document.

Several elements in the tried and reasonably mature approach of the foundations have been to their advantage as they have worked in other countries and with the educational community at home. They have learned to strike a workable balance between adapting to the wants and needs of their clients, while at the same time using their resources creatively and selectively to foster certain areas of development, or to meet emerging problems. For example, both the Rockefeller Foundation and The Ford Foundation recently allocated a number of their grants in health and medicine to assist universities and agencies working in a score of developing nations to conduct research, training, and programs related to family planning and population control. As John Hilliard of The Ford Foundation has pointed out in the American Council on Education's volume, *Universities and Development Assistance Abroad* the foundations can generally avoid entanglement with political forces both at home and abroad. They can be more flexible in their working procedures than official agencies and are able to commit funds for longer periods than most of those agencies. They make mistakes, too, but they provide valuable models for American assistance to education abroad. And they may develop, on the basis of more experience, a philosophy of international development and of the principles and evaluative procedures by which to turn that philosophy into practice.

THE ROLE OF THE AMERICAN EDUCATIONAL COMMUNITY

The American educational community has assisted the growth of international education in numerous ways, some direct, some indirect. In doing so, it has worked in a three-way partnership with agencies and programs of government and with the foundations. As has been indicated, the relationships between the educational institutions and government have been marred by friction and misunderstandings, arising principally from the conflict of governmental and educational procedures and expectations. There has been much more rapport between the universities and colleges and the foundations, for reasons that have also been stated. Following the publication of the Gardner report on *AID and the Universities* in April, 1964, AID undertook to modify its policies and procedures, and the McGovern Bill was introduced, proposing major changes in the policies, organization and technical assistance aspects of foreign aid. Given the magnitude of even the technical assistance aspects of the foreign aid program, one must assume that the elimination of roadblocks and frustrations on both sides will take some time. One must not, however, permit this specific problem of working relationship to obscure the really huge task that has been accomplished by the powerful three-way partnership.

The American colleges and universities have helped greatly to enlarge the world community of scholarship by contributions of knowledge, by strengthening international professional organizations, by the exchange of professional experts, and in many other ways. At the same time they have shouldered major responsibilities for carrying technical and educational assistance to developing countries. With the exception of the assistance given by the Soviet Union in some areas, the contribution of American higher education exceeds that of any other country. The assistance to education has been as diversified as the wide-ranging specific needs of the countries in which it has been given. There have been specific training programs, usually at the request of the receiving countries, in improved rice culture, for example, in public administration, in fiscal management, in planning. There has been assistance in the improvement of library techniques, in the creation of language centers. There has been help to specific faculties and disciplines, and even more to professional schools and institutes. There have been projects to help raise the capacities and standards of whole universities, and even more ambitious projects help better whole educational systems.

The greatest share of this assistance has been channeled through a relatively small number of American universities. In fact, there has been a human tendency on the part of both government agencies and the foundations to call upon and support those universities that have been successful, rather than to broaden the base and assume greater risks of inexperience. With surprising frequency, the universities have sent to tasks abroad some of the ablest members of their faculties, either to work as individuals or as leaders or members of teams. Such has been the demand for manpower in the technical assistance program and such the scarcity of able professors in recent years, however, that the university entrusted with a program has had to recruit from other institutions. This essential practice has had the effect of reducing the benefits which the contracting university derives from the project, since too few of the men and women involved return to the host institution with new knowledge and experience. On the other hand, there has been a wide diffusion of experience, knowledge, and interest that has contributed, particularly at the graduate level, a very genuine and quite professional new international perspective to American higher education.

At present, the American professor who goes abroad for any length of time places his career in jeopardy because overseas service is not equated in terms of promotion with service in the university, and because the overseas professor may have had less chance to do research and publish than his colleagues at home. Some American educators are facing up to this circumstance. Recognizing the mutual value of American assistance abroad to the recipient institutions and to the institution in the United States, they are contemplating, even introducing, ways of equating the service abroad with that at home, and extending to the man or woman on professional leave all of the advantages and emoluments of career development on the campus. Joint appointments in the American university and in one of the universities in the nation where the professor is working are also being proposed as a means toward meeting this problem.

Another means by which the American college and university are contributing to international education is through the exchange of both students and professors. Funds to foster study abroad come from many sources, both public and private. A very substantial proportion of them has come through the Fulbright program which enables American scholars to travel, teach, and conduct research abroad, and in turn brings to the United States outstanding scholars from all over the world. Looked at from the vantage point of the foreign country, the Fulbright program has much to commend it. The recipients of Fulbright grants are normally screened in the country to which they go. They live modestly, at levels closer to those of their indigenous colleagues, than do the representatives of either the foundations or the United States government agencies. Foundation sources, as well as funds from the colleges and universities themselves have made possible the great burgeoning of study abroad by American professors and students. These sources, together with substantial self-support and additional private and government help from their own countries, have made possible the great expansion of study by foreign graduate students and undergraduates at American colleges and universities.

As we consider the impact of the United States educational community on other nations, both developed and developing, it is necessary to look at both sides of the equation; the professors and students who come from abroad to study, teach, or do research, and the Americans who move in the opposite direction for the same purposes. The more direct contribution to the developing nations is to be found, of course, in what United States institutions are able to do for the foreign scholars and students who come here.

Almost eleven thousand foreign professors and other scholars came to the United States in 1966–67 compared with just over 600 twelve years previously. They represented a broad spectrum of nations, even though a third of them continued to come from the United Kingdom, India, and Japan in that order. Almost half were here to work in the sciences, and almost another half were concerned with the humanities, medical sciences, social sciences, and engineering, in that order. Almost all planned to return to their own countries to resume their teaching and research.

During the same year, a record number of more than 100,000 foreign students were at work in American colleges and universities. As with the professors, they came from every part of the world, but in differing proportions. The countries of Asia following prior trends, sent about a third of the total, and of these, two-thirds were graduate students. With the exception of Africa and Oceania, which had fewer students, the other regions—Europe, Latin America, the Near and Middle East, and North America—were reasonably close in numbers, although no one of them had more than half the total of the Asian countries. By contrast with Asia, undergraduates outnumbered graduate students at least three to two from every source except Europe, where the ratio was about even.

To keep the perspective straight, it must be recognized that academic visitors, both students and professors, are welcomed by other countries, and indeed sought by some.

Over a hundred states and territories have recently offered opportunities for cross-national study. Among these, the United Kingdom, France, and Germany are veterans, long visited by students and more mature scholars from all over the world. The Soviet Union has more recently drawn great numbers, particularly from other communist countries and the developing nations, but also from Europe and the United States. Yugoslavia also finances several hundred students from abroad each year. For both professors and students from countries that are not communist, however, the United States continues to be the lodestone, particularly in the sciences.

Simply to have come here to study does not mean, of course, that either the professor or the student has always gained what he sought, that he has genuinely deepened his international understanding, or that he returns to his home happy and prepared to put his new knowledge at the service of his country. Too frequently this has not happened. The record of successful stays and happy departures is higher among the scholars, who would normally find themselves at home anywhere in the world community of scholarship, where there are stimulating colleagues and adequate facilities. The graduate students, who tend to be more purposeful and to come for specific study at particular institutions, are more apt to achieve their ends with satisfaction and to carry home knowledge and experience of value to their own careers and often to their peoples. Undergraduate study offers less assurance of a happy and satisfying outcome and sometimes results, over a period of four years, in a measure of acculturation that will cause the young student difficult problems of readjustment when he returns home. Study abroad at the high school level, as in the American Field Service program, by comparison, has tended to foster enduring attachments to the host country and caused few problems upon the student's return.

A tendency among visiting foreign students to prolong their stays in the United States, and even to remain here in some instances, has caused concern because of the brain drain it may involve, particularly for the developing countries. Stern measures to avoid this outcome were added by the Senate to the International Education Act, and a study of ways to reduce the drain was authorized.

On balance, it must be acknowledged that the American academic community has made a substantial contribution to international education through the opportunities for study and travel it has afforded to foreign students and scholars. They have carried home not only knowledge and skills, but deeper cross-cultural insight, and associations that normally prove to be enduring. Despite all the support brought by the visitors or provided from other sources, the cost to the host institutions has by no means been negligible. On the other hand, no institution that enjoyed the presence of either professors or students from abroad can avoid being aware of the reciprocal advantages they bring to the host college or university. There they become a living force for international perspectives and education.

At this point it should be clear that education must inevitably play a major role in international relations. Both the giving of learning and the hunger and need for it are dynamic forces importantly influencing the intricate and sometimes difficult processes by which peoples and cultures live side by side and interact. It must also be clear that educational assistance holds a priority place in our foreign policy, whether that assistance is rendered abroad or within our own institutions at home. The level of that priority has been very much heightened since the Second World War. Concern about the world and education in it has been both broadened and deepened, and we have expended a considerable amount of our substance and professional talent to give that concern practical meaning. In that measure we have revealed our national awareness of the central role of education in the astounding changes of the latter twentieth century. At the same time, it must be acknowledged that the priority on education, both domestic and international, must be raised even higher. Despite all gains, the need for education and for its constant improvement continues to grow at home and abroad. The pressures of multiplying populations, of urban ills, of drives to eliminate discrimination and to equalize and democratize educational opportunity, together with problems arising from the pollution and potential exhaustion of the world's resources, all heighten the necessity of education. They are piled on top of basic needs that motivated the acceleration of educational effort during the immediate past decades.

Any assessment of the priority to be given international education in foreign policy must be intrinsically an evaluation of its importance to the national interest. There is no denial of that importance by any respected source. There is only competition for the higher claims upon our national resources when the national interest is seen or thought to involve the world patterns of our security. Great expenditures upon war or defense are then given priority, and educational effort is reduced. Wise procedure requires that the relative importance of all the elements essential to the national interest, including education as well as security, be kept under continuous review.

## INTERNATIONAL EDUCATION OF AMERICAN CITIZENS

We shall conclude this essay with an examination of what is being done by the educational community of the United States to equip the present and future citizens of this nation with the capacity to render intelligent and understanding judgments about world relationships and the policies that our nation should pursue in dealing with them. Ideally, the same subject should be described in some manner for every nation in the world. Unfortunately neither space nor available evidence makes this possible. What may be said about the United States, however, could and should be extended in appropriate context to other countries.

Despite some improvements in curriculum and approach in recent years, much too little is done in the schools, colleges and universities to equip the student with a reliable understanding of what the world is and how it works. Although, despite the distressing number of dropouts, there has been a great increase in the proportion of students who attend college and graduate school, very little thought has been given to a sequence of instruction, beginning at the elementary level, that would lead toward a mature, usable knowledge of the structure of the world and its complicated processes of interaction. Although there have been almost startling advances in the disciplines required for international understanding—geography, ethnology, anthropology, history, political science, and others—there are no courses in the "new international relations" in the schools comparable to the "new mathematics" and the "new science." This is in part due to the scarcity of university centers in which cross-disciplinary approaches are either in use or are being developed and tested. In part, the failure is due to insufficient articulation between even the elementary and secondary schools, and to the frequent lack of it between the high schools and the colleges. A splendid opportunity exists for a group of competent and dedicated scholars and teachers to make a real breakthrough in the American educational system that might provide models for other countries. As they do so, they will find awaiting their examination a very few experimental courses designed to accomplish these purposes. One of them, developed at a western college, specifically aims to help the student learn what questions to ask about any society undergoing modernization, and regards the techniques and skills involved as transferrable from one culture to another. Not all the models will be found in the United States, by any means. As the scholars and teachers probe for experience that will be helpful to them in the development of sequential courses, or combinations of courses, they will do well to explore what other countries are doing.

At the high school level, and even more at the college level, one must think not only in terms of a single interdisciplinary course, but also in terms of appropriate sequences of courses among the several disciplines. Again, the development of model curricula is of high priority. It need scarcely be said that within such curricula and the courses comprising them, the emphasis should be upon not only the acquisition of knowledge, but, more importantly, upon skills of analysis, interpretation, and synthesis. The objective should be a mind equipped to think in cross-cultural and international terms, and to know what foundations of fact and interpretation are essential to reliable judgments.

The needs just described are, of course, intrinsic to a general or liberal education. They are designed essentially for the undergraduate college, inside or outside the university. The importance of the needs is pointed up by the data assembled by the Department of Health, Education, and Welfare, and cited earlier in this chapter in connection with the International Education Act. This survey made evident that a predominant number of colleges and universities have inadequate offerings and requirements in the international field. They also make evident, by contrast, that a minority of institutions is making excellent progress in the development of courses and curricula at the undergraduate level. The experience of a broad sampling is made available in a publication of the Association of American Colleges entitled *Non-Western Studies in the Liberal Arts College.* Philosophies of undergraduate study, together with specific recommendations concerning the resources that may be drawn upon, are contained in the Morrill report, *The Universities and World Affairs,* and the Nason report, on *The College and World Affairs,* both available through Education and World Affairs.

Great strides have been taken by American universities toward the development of international study centers, and toward ample graduate work on specific countries and regions, sometimes within departments, sometimes in area programs of an interdisciplinary character. The International Education Act, when it is financed, will make possible the further development of existing international study centers, and the creation of new ones. It will facilitate the much-needed multiplication of opportunities for area and language study at both the graduate and undergraduate levels.

In the larger universities with well-developed area programs and advanced graduate work on particular countries there is often strong emphasis upon specialization. Some graduate departments and institutes wish to see this specialization begin in the later years of undergraduate work, and some four year colleges concur in this judgment. There is normally, and with justification, a demand for early language training for those who aspire to become specialists. Inevitably this has involved conflict between specialization and the concepts of general education or liberal education, most of which aim to use the four years of undergraduate education for the development of the "well-educated person" to whom reference was made earlier in this essay. It also conflicts potentially with the cultivation of knowledge and skills essential to wise citizenship. It is probable that no satisfactory compromise between these two approaches will be reached, but rather that an uneasy accommodation will be found and maintained.

The educated citizen, whoever he may be, cannot escape the necessity of participating in the policy decisions of his government, even if he does so negatively as a recluse. In recent years the process of decision making has been intensively studied. Much more is known about it, although the research must still be regarded as being in its initial stage. Even though it may not prove possible or desirable in the schools and colleges to offer anything as complicated as the systems analysis approach to decision (although such a possibility cannot be excluded), the simple elements of the decision process can be offered and learned. At some few institutions they are being provided and, in fact, made fascinating by use of simulation techniques. In the matter of decision making, as in learning about the world, there is serious need to bring together in reasonable compass a record of the experience already available, and to provide for the broadening of both knowledge and experience through workshops, seminars, and other methods.

It is within the context of the preparation of American youth to participate wisely in the foreign and domestic decisions of their government bearing upon international relations that it is appropriate to consider their study abroad and that of their professors. Such study is, in reality, an extension of work on the campus, an extension wholly consonant with the urgent quest for relevance that characterizes today's generations of students. Obviously, the very presence abroad of both scholars and students is itself an effective factor in the international process. For these reasons, if for no other, the travel and study abroad emanating from American campuses should meet standards of excellence equal to or better than those exacted in any part of the home institutions.

In comparison with the almost 11,000 foreign professors and other scholars who came to the United States in 1966–67, some 4600 of their American colleagues went abroad to study. The largest proportion went to Europe, but there was a significant scattering on other continents. Half were in the humanities and social sciences, and almost 19% more in the sciences. The professional schools provided fewer. This is understandable, given the state of the several disciplines in the United States and elsewhere. Moreover, the pattern has prevailed for some time. It does have one unfortunate effect, however, from the standpoint of the international education of young Americans. They have less opportunity for exposure to scholars who have lived and studied in Asia, the Middle East, Africa, and Latin America than to those who have been in Europe. This is regrettable principally because of the importance which these developing regions will have for us in the future.

The same observations apply to students from American institutions going abroad. There were about one fourth as many in 1965–66 as there were foreign students coming here. With the exception of Mexico, certain other Latin American countries, and Canada, Japan, the Philippines, and Israel, the bulk went to Europe. Like their professors, they were predominantly interested in the humanities and social sciences, although in their case the proportion of interest in the medical sciences exceeded that in the pure sciences.

Much could be said about the study of American students abroad, because it has been subjected to careful scrutiny, and much has been written about it. It is sufficient to state that study abroad, under proper circumstances, can be a very important part of the preparation of young Americans for deeper international understanding and responsible citizenship. It does not always attain this potential because there is wide variation in the quality of the programs conducted abroad. There is also variation in the degree of integration between the period of foreign study and work on the home campus. Some programs are highly imaginative and excellent. Some fall far behind. And finally it must be observed that there have as yet been very few adequate evaluations of the impact of study abroad on either the individual, or upon the college or university to which he returns.

A very special case of overseas education and experience for American youth is the Peace Corps. As of June, 1966 there were over 8000 Peace Corps Volunteers engaged in teaching. They and their fellow volunteers in other enterprises, are located all over the world, but principally in the developing countries. The program was begun in 1961 and has won support, not only from the Congress and the American public, but also from nations to which the volunteers have been sent upon request. In fact, the impact of this small band of dedicated American youth to the processes of international relations has been out of all proportion to their number. Living as they have had to live at the level of the peoples among whom they work, they have gained a far from superficial insight into other cultures and ways of life. Their influence upon American higher education, both through the training programs mounted for them, and by what they have brought back to graduate work and teaching has also been of a magnitude and importance exceeding their numbers.

## Conclusion

We conclude where we began, with the assumption that education must play a critical role in the great network of change of epochal dimension that is transforming the world. Hopefully, the fact and argument presented in this essay will have demonstrated that this assumption is not a cliché, but rather a hard international reality. Without being an alarmist or Cassandra, it is possible to reiterate again in all sincerity the dire prophesy of H. G. Wells that the future is a race between education and catastrophe.

When one faces both the assumption and the prophecy, there is a temptation to rush for panaceas and instant solutions. Hopefully we have grown sufficiently mature to recognize that these are but wisps of the impossible, spun of unnecessary desperation and impatience. A more workmanlike approach is needed. The hard and tough task of building programs of education that will yield greater understanding of the world and of what it demands of us and of others, will be hammered out by thought, by research, by intelligent planning, and by trial and error. Our progress will be essentially pragmatic in design as we confront one by one the realities within our own nation and in others, as we estimate the forces upon which we can count, the tools we can use, which persons we can trust to get what done. Our work will inevitably have political overtones. In our strategy, therefore, we shall have to learn how to circumvent political as well as bureaucratic and economic roadblocks, while attempting to keep our direction true and our goal in sight.

The work to be done will be in the book-lined office of a professor, a dean, or a college president. It will be in the office of a foundation officer, who will mask his enthusiasm for a project with the conventional language of restraint. It will be in an office of a federal department, and it will be in the halls of the Congress and of the State Legislatures. It will be in a ministry of education overseas or in the committee rooms of a national study group. It will be in the sanctuary of the president or vice-chancellor of a foreign university, and in the less pretentious quarters of those who guide parts of the institution. It will be in the small office of a village school principal, in the more elaborate office network of a great urban school system. It will be at the centers of industry and commerce and in the several headquarters of the press, radio, and television. It will be at the centers of both international and regional organizations. And in the midst of urgency, the task will often seem inordinately slow and plodding. Patience and the capacity to wait there must be, but also the skillful and delicate capacity to obtain, without offense, more efficiency, more sense of the great importance of the job, more capacity to translate that sense of importance from words into concrete achievements. These there must be because history will not wait, any more than it will be hurried.

Pragmatic as the task must be, it must also be conceived in grand rather than mean dimensions. For the requirements of the times will not be met with less than grand conceptions. There must be a guiding sense of the wholeness and inter-relatedness of the effort to improve education everywhere and for all peoples, a wholeness dictated by the common nature of the adventure, whatever differences in detail there may be, and even more by the obligation of civilized man to man.

An excellent start in the direction of wholeness presiding over particularization has been made in the International Education Act. When implemented, it will mobilize, as never before, the educational resources of this nation to prepare our present and future citizens to live in the world as well as in this country. It will prepare young men and women not only to live with but also to work with their peers in other nations and in international bodies. It rests upon an assumption that there is an inescapable wholeness about the world as well as about education in that world. And it then proceeds to state, one by one, steps that can be taken to realize that wholeness.

Other countries have had to think in whole terms also. Some of the younger developing ones have done so boldly, as they have found it necessary to place the detailed needs of their educational systems in a conceptual framework of what their countries must do to meet the present and future requirements of a modernized nation, as they have sought ways to live without ignorance or poverty or fear of aggression or destruction.

It is now practical to plan universal adjuncts to education, based upon the use of communication satellites. In fact, the planning is going forward. The potential of this new instrument for great good or evil is almost as sobering as that of nuclear fission. Even if there were not other compelling reasons to elevate our sight to the vision of what education on a world scale could mean, the prospect of being able to reach the eyes and ears of students everywhere from what might be a single source should give us pause. It is a prospect that demands a profound sense of responsibility to young minds and to human values. It is a responsibility that can be served and respected only by men and nations who have given thought to what universality in education can and should mean, and stand ready to implement and defend their conclusions in a world still fraught with political conflict. Once more, advancing technology may be rendering obsolete vestigial beliefs that education can be conceived in less than world terms, or that it can have anything less than an integral place and a high priority in foreign policy.

By good fortune, this imperative coincides with a dream that begins to appear realizable, that education up to the highest levels can be made available to the whole of humanity. If the pace of history will permit this to happen effectively, there will be hope for the world.

# 4. *International Cooperation and the Two Faces of Science*

## *ROGER REVELLE*

*Many shall run to and fro,*
*and knowledge shall be increased.*
— DANIEL 12.4

### THE TWO ASPECTS OF SCIENCE

Science has two aspects: one is the search for truth—
the attempt to gain understanding of the world about us
and of ourselves; the other is the use of knowledge to gain
control over nature and power over men.

### *The search for truth*

In its aspect of the search for truth, international cooperation in science is a contradiction in terms. The search for
truth is not national, it is personal and individual; hence,
it cannot be international in the sense of relations among
nations. The work of individual scientists finds its meaning in the context of the work of their predecessors, their
contemporaries, and their successors throughout the community of science. This community cuts across national
boundaries, and, indeed, is as wide as the great globe itself,
just as its objects of study are as wide as the universe.

Nor is scientific excellence the exclusive possession of any
one nation or group of nations; the talents and capabilities
of scientists in many lands constitute a valuable resource
for all nations. Cooperation among scientists of different
countries in the search for truth is, therefore, as old as
science. The language, methods, and ethics of this search
are universal; its only limitations are those of the human

mind. Because of the unity and interdependence of science, it transcends differences in political and social systems and is supra-national.

The supra-national values that guide scientists in their search for truth conflict at times with the foreign policies of nations; resolution of these conflicts calls for a high order of statesmanship. Cooperation in scientific truth-seeking can be a powerful tool for building international understanding only if its cohesive force is aided by national attitudes, policies, and actions.

In the search for truth, a structure of world-wide working relationships among scientists is essential in such major areas of inquiry as geophysics, meteorology, oceanography, animal and human ecology, astrophysics, and public health. These sciences take most meaningful form only on a global framework. Hurricanes, droughts, and pestilence know no national boundaries.

The world contains phenomena far beyond what is available within any single country, and distant parts of the earth must be the stage for much scientific research. In botany, for example, a transect around the world along the 45th parallel would constitute virtually a controlled experiment. In this latitude lie such diverse environments as the vineyards of Bordeaux, the smiling valley of the Po, the mouths of the Danube, the Crimean beach resorts of the Soviet Union, Mongolia's Gobi Desert, and the northern tip of Japan's frigid island of Hokkaido. In the United States, the 45th parallel stretches from the mild and rainy coast of Oregon across the plains of Dakota to the tip of Maine. These various environments have one thing in common—the number of hours of daylight and darkness at different seasons throughout the year. Yet there are several species of cosmopolitan plants that reproduce naturally in many places, but only near this latitude. Evidently, their specific character is determined by photoperiodism, and not by temperature or humidity, or other climatic factors.

### Control over nature

Science has another purpose besides striving for truth: this is control over the forces of nature, hopefully for the welfare of mankind. It is a truism to say that in our times the applications of science and technology are exerting a revolutionary influence on men and nations. Science and technology today give power, not only over the external world, but also over other human beings. This is the chief reason why the leaders of modern governments are concerned with science. The sovereigns of the Middle Ages employed alchemists in a desperate attempt to replenish their empty treasuries; the governments of today support research largely because a continually advancing technology is essential for military security and economic growth.

In this aspect of their work, scientists are primarily citizens. Their discoveries determine the policies of governments, and governments, in turn, profoundly influence the course of science.

In the enlightened 18th century, a learned man could separate his scientific work from his political life. Benjamin Franklin must have been thinking as a Fellow of the Royal Society, even though he was Postmaster General of the revolting Colonies, when he issued an order that American ships should give aid and comfort to Captain James Cook. Lavoisier's head was cut off because he was on the wrong side politically, even while the world honored him for his chemical discoveries.

Few scientists in our era of scientific revolution can search for truth from an ivory tower. In their work, as in their lives, they must first be citizens of a country. To a greater degree than ever before, they are in the position of Socrates when he heard humming in his ears, like the sound of the flute in the ears of the mystic, the voices of the law that kept him from hearing any other as they said, "He who disobeys us is, as we maintain, thrice wrong. . . ."

### Science and politics

Even if they wanted to, today's scientists could not be indifferent to public affairs; their welfare and their opportunities for accomplishment are too closely interwoven with the lives of nations and the world of politics. As a consequence, many scientists are having to assume a quasi-political role.

This is not to say that modern politics and modern science are the same thing; on the contrary, they rest on quite different foundations. Science proceeds step-wise from the known to the unknown, transferring at each step from the particular to the general and back again, building at each step a model of understanding that can be used to generalize, to unify, and to predict. The successful scientist attacks only those problems he feels able to solve, problems on the frontier of knowledge but ready for solution. The politician deals always with the unknown future. He cannot select problems that are solvable; his problems are thrust upon him by the force of events. He must base his actions not on rational understanding but on experience and insight. He deals with intangibles, with the mysteries of human motives and emotions; he can see only a short distance into the future, and, even so, through a glass darkly.

The essence of politics is that it deals with particular problems, not with generalities, and with unique problems that are never exactly the same as those that have arisen before. The results of political action are always uncertain; the effective politician must always be prepared to alter his actions in the light of events. He knows better than most scientists that men do not behave reasonably, but in accordance with the patterns of their culture, that the human mind is not the logical machine described by Aristotle, but follows quite different and, as yet, unknown laws.

From the political standpoint of today, international cooperation in science and technology should have many virtues. In former times, mutual understanding between scientists of different countries had little relevance for the mass of their compatriots. Now scientists in their quasi-political roles can contribute effectively toward elimination of suspicion and prejudice. More important, international cooperation provides the free exchange of ideas that is essential for rapid technical progress. Politicians and diplomats have gradually come to a partial understanding of these facts. But in their nation-structured world, the scientist, like the artist, is bound to be suspect because of the supra-national nature of his interests. How can a man who believes that truth is universal, while he is at the same time skeptical about his own possession of it, be trusted to be single-mindedly loyal to one nation? Moreover, statesmen look with marked distaste on the fact that their most cherished and time-tested policies can be nullified by scientific discoveries they can neither control nor predict.

Today, as in the recent past, the secrecy imposed by national security considerations impedes much potential international cooperation in science, even though it can be argued from the history of atomic weapons that secrecy does not guarantee security. The suspicions engendered by secrecy may in fact lead to a dangerous instability in the precarious equilibrium of terror under which we live. An open world may be the only world that can survive in a technological age.

### Expanding science and shrinking world

Science itself, both as truth-seeker and as controller of nature, has contributed to the widespread recognition of the need for cooperation among nations. Jet aircraft and high-speed communication have shrunk the human world. The astronauts and the International Geophysical Year have helped men everywhere to feel in their bellies, not just on the edges of their minds, that the earth is a space-ship, isolated and complete in itself, and that we who travel on it must work together if we are to survive.

The accelerating changes brought about by technology are obvious to everyone, but the growth of the scientific enterprise that has produced these changes is little known. Yet, in advanced countries during recent years the numbers of scientists and technicians have been doubling every decade.

Of course, other forms of human activity, as well as the total numbers of human beings, are also increasing, but at a slower rate. The doubling times are 15 to 40 years. Such a difference can hardly be maintained for very long.

At the beginning of the 19th century, the total number of scientific and technical journals was roughly 100; by 1850 it reached about 1,000; by 1900 it was 10,000. Now it is 100,000. If the rate of growth continues, we may expect a million scientific periodicals before the end of this century. This exponential proliferation of scientific information menaces the unity, and, hence the very existence, of science as we have known it. Science is in danger of a kind of suicide either by self-suffocation or by tearing itself into isolated fragments.

## KINDS OF SCIENTIFIC COOPERATION

Like every aspect of science, scientific cooperation across national boundaries has burgeoned mightily during the last twenty years, and we have learned a good deal about its blessings and defects.

The most important and valuable kind of cooperation is simply that which improves communication among scientists of different countries. This can take many forms: organization and support of international congresses, conferences, and symposia; establishment of international scientific journals, and abstracting and translating services; direct exchange of persons, from graduate students to senior scientists; facilitation of such exchanges by compiling directories and publicizing opportunities, as well as by financial support; exchanges of data which can be used to test hypotheses and theories; exchanges of instruments and techniques; development of the specialized languages of science by international agreements on nomenclature and the definition of terms.

### International scientific meetings

Since World War II, all these aids to communication have greatly increased. For example, it has been estimated that each year between 15,000 and 20,000 United States scientists and engineers attend several hundred international meetings where they have personal contact with tens of thousands of their colleagues from other countries.

Face-to-face meetings among scientists, whether in each other's laboratories, in informal symposia, or in international congresses, are a most effective means for exchange of scientific information and ideas. One of the reasons such meetings are essential is the overwhelming tide of scientific publications described above, which forces even the most rapid reader to concentrate on a microscopically narrow range of interest. But there are at least three other reasons.

The first, not generally recognized by laymen, is the fact that good art and good science have much in common. Both depend on a seeing eye and on imagination. The artist and the scientist must be able to see things that other people do not see, and to find relationships, through the free association we call imagination, between things that have never been related before. As with many arts, a good deal of science cannot be communicated, much less taught, except through direct personal contact. This is particularly true of experimental techniques. Details of experimental procedure are hard to describe in words and are rarely published; they must be seen to be believed.

The second reason is also contrary to common belief: scientific ideas are usually born in conversation, rather than in the mind of one man. The rigorous thinking needed to nurse a new-born idea into a useful hypothesis must almost always be done in private. But the fresh insights, the new associations between previously unrelated phenomena, often come from the interplay of two or three minds clashing in conversation.

Even more important is the fact that, in talking face to face, scientists allow themselves to state their intuitions and partly-formulated ideas, unconstrained by the caution they demand in the printed word. Custom requires that the usual scientific meeting shall center around a series of formal papers. But just as graduate students often learn more from each other than from their professors, so mature scientists learn from informal discussion in the lobby as much as from the lecture in the auditorium.

### Exchange of students and research workers

Exchange of scientists at its best implies free movement across national boundaries for study, teaching, research, and the sharing of knowledge.

At present, American and mainland Chinese scientists are virtually cut off from each other, and only the first steps toward free exchange have been taken in the relations between the United States and the Soviet Union. The National Academy of Sciences of the United States and the Academy of Sciences of the U.S.S.R. have a tenuous agreement under which a few scientists of various levels of distinction and experience are exchanged each year on a *quid pro quo* basis. In comparison with the total numbers of foreign students and faculty members in the United States and the corresponding numbers of Americans abroad, the extent of exchanges with the Soviet Union is infinitesimal. According to *Open Doors 1967*, published by the Institute of International Education, out of the 100,262 foreign students in the United States in 1966–67, 56 were from the U.S.S.R.; 31 out of 24,900 American overseas students attended Soviet educational institutions. Of the 10,737 faculty members from other countries who spent a major part of the year in the United States, 16 were Soviet citizens. Of the 4,674 American university faculty members who taught and did research abroad, only 26 made an extended visit to the U.S.S.R. Ten of these were social scientists, eight were in the humanities, seven were from the physical and life sciences, and one was an engineer. The total numbers of students and faculty members involved in Soviet-American exchanges has grown very little over the past six years.

In contrast, on a worldwide and overall basis the numbers of foreign students and faculty members in the United States, and the numbers of Americans overseas have been rapidly increasing. In 1966–67, 111,000 foreign citizens studied or did research at American universities, colleges, and hospitals. This was an increase of 114 percent over 1957. The number of foreign faculty members and advanced researchers on United States campuses was more than nine times the number in 1957. United States faculty members abroad increased three fold in ten years—from 1,492 in 1956–57 to 4,674 in 1966–67.

Of the 111,000 foreign citizens in the United States, 90 percent were students at 1,797 American universities and colleges—41 percent as undergraduates, and 49 percent as graduates or special students.

The number of American scholars overseas was less than a third of the number of foreign citizens on American campuses. Five hundred and sixty-four institutions in 82 foreign countries were hosts to United States students, and American faculty members from 650 universities and colleges taught or carried out research in 124 countries.

Analysis of these figures shows some marked imbalances. Although United States institutions in 50 states, the District of Columbia, Puerto Rico, and Guam reported foreign students on their campuses, more than half of these students were in 58 universities. Woodbury College in Los Angeles had the highest proportion, with one out of five of its student body being from overseas; the proportion was one out of six at Howard University, and one out of eight at MIT. In some southern universities, there were two hundred American students for one from outside the United States.

Only between the United States and Western Europe is there a genuine two-way flow of scholars and students. During 1966–67, 18,678 Europeans studied or taught in the United States, and 16,940 Americans worked in the Western European countries. In contrast, 72 percent of the foreign students and scholars in the United States came from the Far East, Latin America, the Near and Middle East, and Africa, while only about a third of the Americans went to these areas. There were 110 times as many Chinese in the United States as Americans in Taiwan and Hong Kong, 40 times as many Indians in the United States as Americans in India, and 4 times as many Japanese here as Americans in Japan. On the other hand, there were four times more Americans in France than Frenchmen in the United States, and twice as many Americans in Switzerland and Austria.

About 47 percent of the foreign students on United States campuses majored in engineering, natural and physical sciences, medicine, or agriculture, 20 percent in the humanities, and 15 percent in the social sciences. Over half of the American students abroad were concerned with the humanities, including creative and liberal arts, languages, literature, and theology, and only about 30 percent with sciences, medicine, engineering, and agriculture. The attraction of the United States for persons interested in the sciences and related fields is also seen in the figures for foreign faculty members in this country, of whom 74 percent were in the natural and physical sciences, medicine, engineering, and agriculture. Only 22 percent of the American scholars overseas were in these fields.

The distribution of students by fields of study on a worldwide basis, as revealed by *Study Abroad,* published by UNESCO in 1966, is similar to that of foreign students in the United States. About 13 percent in 1964 were in the natural sciences, 16 percent in medicine, 18 percent in engineering, and 3 percent in agriculture, giving a total of 51 percent in scientific and technical fields, compared with 19 percent who were studying law or social sciences, and 24 percent in humanities and education.

The U.S.S.R. does not publish any data on the countries of origin of its foreign students or on their fields of study, only that in 1964 they came from 110 countries. However, such data are available from Czechoslovakia, where 67 percent of the students were in the natural sciences, engineering, medicine, or agriculture, and 13 percent were in the social sciences. As in the United States, other countries report very small numbers of students from the Soviet Union. But there were 39 Soviet students in the Vatican in 1960–61, more than the number in the United States for the same year.

More than half of the 300,000 foreign students in the world's universities and colleges are at least partly supported by fellowships and travel grants; 170,000 such awards were reported to UNESCO in 1964–65—over eleven times the number in 1948–49. The number of fellowships is now doubling every five to six years. Five percent of these are offered by the United Nations and other international organizations, 45 percent by governments, and the remainder by foundations, educational institutions, and other private organizations. As might be expected, the largest proportion of fellowship programs, 30 percent (1961), is in basic and applied sciences, but about 25 percent of all programs are not restricted to any particular field.

Over 300 universities and colleges in the United States and nearly 200 foundations, ranging from the Texas-Swedish Cultural Foundation to the Institute of World Affairs, offer some 56,000 fellowships of which about 18 percent are abroad by United States citizens and over 80 percent for study in the United States by citizens of other countries. Many of these are for undergraduate or graduate students, but others, such as the fellowship in Mammalian Biology offered by the National Academy of Sciences—National Research Council, are for post-doctoral research workers, or, even, in some cases, for middle-aged scientists. The number of fellowships available in the National Academy program is unspecified, but presumably large, while in others, such as that of the Women's Auxiliary to the American Society of Mechanical Engineers, only one fellowship is offered.

It may be of interest to academic administrators to note

that the student-faculty ratio of foreign citizens in the United States is about 10 to 1, whereas the ratio of American students to American faculty members abroad is only 5 to 1. If these ratios remain constant while the total number of exchanges continues its exponential rise, American faculty members left at home may soon start to complain about their added teaching loads.

On the other hand, the excess numbers of foreign students and scholars in the United States over their American counterparts abroad constitute an important "invisible" export, which contributes to our foreign exchange earnings, and thus helps to restore the balance of payments deficit. If the proportion of foreign scientists to Americans can be maintained as the numbers keep rising, the unfavorable effects of tourism on the United States balance of payments may be significantly alleviated. Although part of their living costs are paid for by grants from the United States government or by private American funds, students and scholars stay here for a much longer time and spend more money per head than the average tourist.

From a less provincial point of view, the imbalance between foreign students and scholars in the United States and the number of Americans abroad has a serious consequence for other countries. At least 10 percent of these visitors remain permanently in the United States, and thus become part of the so-called "brain drain." This is a worldwide phenomenon, which lays its heaviest burden on the poor countries. The enormous technological superiority of Europe and North America and their ever-growing requirements for highly educated technologists act as a magnet to pull away the ablest and best educated persons from the less advanced countries. The problem is compounded, and to a considerable extent created by the difficulties faced by scientists, engineers and other professionally trained young people in finding meaningful opportunities to use their acquired knowledge and skills in their own countries. This brings into sharp focus the conflict between the two aspects of science. To advance the search for truth, scientists need to work in the environment of sophisticated instruments and stimulating colleagues that exists in the advanced countries; but to help with economic and social development, their presence is most needed where the greatest problems are, and this is in the less developed countries.

One way to reconcile these conflicting needs has been pioneered by the International Atomic Energy Agency in the establishment of the International Institute of Theoretical Physics at Trieste. Under the leadership of the famous Pakistan physicist, Abdus Salam, the Institute brings theoretical physicists from the poor countries together for conferences and workshops of three months to a year with colleagues from the advanced countries, and thereby enables them to contribute to and remain in intimate contact with the cutting edge of their science, while still serving in the universities and laboratories of their own countries.

A large part of the brain drain, notably in medicine and engineering, results from another factor: the failure of the advanced countries to educate enough physicians and other specialists for their own needs. To the extent that this is so, the rich countries are literally obtaining a kind of reverse technical assistance from the poor ones, at a cost, to the latter, in monetary terms alone, of hundreds of millions of dollars a year.

### Other forms of cooperation

Other forms of cooperation include observations and measurements of phenomena that cut across national boundaries or are worldwide in nature. Careful planning, continuous communication, and free exchange of data are essential for success, especially when the measurements must be relatively simultaneous. The International Geophysical Year, described in some detail below, was an example of this kind of cooperation.

In all fields of science, it has long been recognized that standards of measurement and methods of observation must be inter-calibrated on an international basis. The rise of many new sciences and technologies has multiplied the problem in recent years.

Some experimental instruments, such as the high-energy particle accelerator of modern physics, are not only inordinately expensive, but extremely difficult to construct and operate. International cooperation in financing and utilizing accelerators has been quite successful at the European

Center for Nuclear Research (CERN), and accelerators in the United States and the U.S.S.R. have also been made available to scientists of various nations.

## Cooperation in Technical Assistance

Technical assistance comprises those measures, short of the provision of significant capital, undertaken by a technically advanced country or inter-governmental organization to develop the human and natural resources and technical capabilities of a less advanced country. The concept in its modern form is only about twenty years old, though it has roots in colonial and missionary practices. Scientific research and the analytical methods of science have not been used to the maximum in any technical assistance programs, most of which have been in the hands of educators, engineers, and others concerned with short-term goals. Research is generally of limited usefulness in solving short-range problems, though modern methods of analysis of these problems could be better utilized than they have been.

Short-term problems often seem critically important, but the ultimate purpose of technical assistance must be the long-range one of helping other nations to achieve an economic, political, and social transformation into free and viable communities in a modern world. In each of the poor countries this transformation is impeded by major problems—both long-standing and emergent—which require well-documented experimentation or other kinds of applied research for their solution.

While some technical assistance programs have been notably successful, the results of others have been disappointing. Among the reasons for limited success has been lack of knowledge about such factors as the nature of change in societies, and its dependence and effects upon individuals and upon the structure and mores of the society; inadequate means for effective communication of skills and ideas between different societies and cultures; and the limited applicability of technologies developed under one set of conditions to markedly different situations.

It has been possible to triple the yield of wheat on large farms in Mexico by using improved seed, chemical fertilizers, and better agricultural practices. But these measures have been relatively ineffective under the conditions of small farm plots and archaic land tenure in Iran. Applied research on the coastal fisheries of Peru, sponsored by the U.N. Special Fund and undertaken by the Food and Agriculture Organization is notably successful. But the attempt to introduce Norwegian scientific fisheries methods off the coast of Kerala in India has been impeded by the lack of repair facilities for motorized fishing vessels and the difficulties of developing a market for the catch. The Helmand River Dam in Afghanistan is a monument to skilled engineering, but part of the lands brought under irrigation are deteriorating because of waterlogging and salination of the soil. Much valuable technical equipment has been distributed to educational institutions in the less developed countries. But a good deal of it no longer works, either because skilled repair and maintenance men are not available or because no one on the staff of the recipient institution has a scientific problem which requires the use of the equipment. Plants for production of antibiotics and other highly technical products have been built in some developing countries, but because they are isolated from an industrial complex and usually operate far below capacity, the cost of production may be as much as ten times higher than that of comparable products in the advanced countries.

In attempting to improve the policies and practices of technical assistance, research and development can enlarge our body of knowledge and skill. The whole spectrum of the natural, social, and behavioral sciences should be utilized to gain understanding of the nature of transition in developing areas and to forecast the effectiveness of assistance programs.

### New technologies for the developing countries

Much modern technology must be simplified to be useful to developing countries. New technologies suited to available energy sources, environment, and economic and social patterns must often be developed. To meet the specific needs of particular countries or regions, substantial efforts should also be devoted to devising adaptations from the vast store of modern scientific and technical knowledge. This adaptive research must usually be performed in the area or region concerned. In any case, the problems must be identified and the proposed solutions must be tested there.

These countries are overwhelmingly rural, and one of their key problems is that of electrical or mechanical energy in the villages. What can modern science and technology offer the villager to lighten his toil and strengthen his hands, within the means he can afford? The diffuseness of the market for energy in the villages makes supply in modern forms a difficult problem.

There are numerous problems of public health in tropical countries. Radically cheapening the purification of water would be of great benefit. So would simple, culturally acceptable outdoor latrines and indoor toilets not requiring running water. Applications of nutritional knowledge, particularly to the problems of protein deficiency in human diets, are urgently needed to aid the proper growth of children and improve the health of adults. Simple methods of refrigeration for food storage and for cooling of houses would help in nutrition by reducing food wastage.

To lift agriculture above the subsistence level, abundant, cheap, and properly regulated water is needed for irrigation. Applied research and development should be conducted on means for location of underground water, drilling and pumping of wells, prevention of evaporation losses in reservoirs and in the farmers' fields, inexpensive lining of irrigation canals to prevent seepage, desalination of water, and higher-yielding, salt-tolerant crops.

In nearly all low-income countries, rapid population growth absorbs a major part of increases in production, and slows the pace of development. The importance of biological research on less expensive and more effective methods of contraception than now exist, and of sociological and psychological investigations of the barriers to population control, cannot be over-emphasized.

Some facets of the research needs of the low income countries can be met in the laboratories of the scientifically advanced nations, but most of the research must be done locally in order to meet local conditions. This means that building up research capabilities within these countries is fundamental to technical progress.

The barriers separating the academic world of more or less "pure" science from the world of everyday action in agriculture, industry, health, and social problems tend to be particularly great in the less developed countries. Their scientists and engineers need the encouragement and example of western colleagues in research collaboration on their urgent applied problems.

### Institutional relationships

One of the organizational patterns by which the scientific research communities of technologically advanced countries can contribute to the progress of developing countries is through long-term inter-institutional cooperation.

Such relationships need especially to be arranged between western universities and the universities of the less advanced countries, particularly those that are being newly established or reformed. They can include a systematic interchange of faculty, research staff, and graduate students, joint selection of problems and assignment of priorities for research, searching out and drawing upon existing scientific and technological knowledge, bringing to bear specialized scientific talent and equipment not otherwise available to the newly developing country, and collaboration in methods for bridging the gap between research and practical action.

Successful examples of such relationships are those between North Carolina State University and the Agricultural University at Los Molinos in Peru, and between the Cornell University College of Agriculture and the College of Agriculture of the University of the Philippines.

A consortium of American technical schools and universities helped to organize and provide long-term help for the Indian Institute of Technology at Kanpur in India. This is one of five such Indian Institutes, each of which has been assisted by a different country or intergovernmental agency, including West Germany, the United Kingdom, U.S.S.R., and UNESCO. On a smaller scale, Washington State University is working with the Agricultural University at Lyallpur in West Pakistan, and Texas A & M College assists the Engineering University at Dacca in East Pakistan. Many more examples could be given. Similar relationships exist among governmental scientific agencies, such as those between the United States Geological Survey and the corresponding natural resources agencies in several South American countries, and between the French Organization for Overseas Scientific and Technical Research (ORSTOM), and scientific institutions in some of the former French colonies.

### Technical Consultants

Many projects for development of natural resources and industry in the poor countries require a greater volume or higher level of technical competence than is available locally. These needs are supplied in part by special consultants from intergovernmental agencies, including the World Bank, FAO, WHO, and UNESCO, and in part by private consulting firms or non-profit organizations. Several dozen European and American firms specialize in this activity and have built up large field- and home-office staffs. These are usually heavily weighted with engineers and former colonial officers and tend to lack the multidisciplinary outlook necessary for comprehensive analysis of country problems, but they have proven very helpful and indeed necessary in feasibility studies and design of individual projects.

### Regional research centers

The Ford and Rockefeller Foundations as well as some governmental and intergovernmental agencies have established regional research centers for agriculture, human nutrition or health in different parts of the less developed world. Perhaps the most successful of these is the International Rice Research Institute at Los Banos in the Philippines. This Ford- and Rockefeller-supported, internationally staffed institution has developed, through genetic and agronomic research, new varieties of fast-maturing rice which can yield more than ten times as much grain per acre per year as the indigenous varieties in the paddy fields of South Asia. These new varieties are now being widely adopted in India and other neighboring countries and may completely change the level of food supplies and the nature of agriculture in these countries.

### Development of scientific participation

The values and methods of science must be woven into the fabric of any society that is to be viable in the modern world. No country can afford to rely entirely on technical advice from foreign specialists, who are bound to be unfamiliar with its broadest and deepest problems. In our era of revolutionary technical change each country should have its own recognized scientists who have the sophistication, insight, and self-confidence to be able to evaluate the potentialities of technical innovations in the context of their own society. More important, the traditional and static social structures of the less advanced countries must be leavened with the spirit of rational inquiry, the recognition of uncertainty, and the patient, hard-working optimism of science. Finally, no country that fails to contribute at least in a small way to the advance of scientific understanding can in the long run participate fully and with dignity in the economic and social benefits of scientific discovery. Some developing countries recognize these facts and have sought advice in establishing their own programs of scientific research and development.

The developing countries need material assistance as well as advice if they are to participate in modern science. Even in such a relatively advanced country as India, there is a sad scarcity of scientific books and periodicals, scientific instruments, and biological reference collections. Instruments on hand are often out of service because spare parts are not available. Easily accessible funds for instrument repairs and replacement are of vital importance.

Equally serious in the poorer countries is the lack of jobs—and status—for young scientists. Many American faculty members have helped with the advanced education of young people from these countries who have later reported their lack of opportunity to use their specialized training back at home. Some have had to find work entirely outside science simply to keep their families alive.

Foundations or government agencies for the support of free research proposed by scientists themselves, analogous to the National Science Foundation in the United States, exist in few countries. Consequently, young scientists in most regions of the world struggle against great odds in following their own scientific imaginations and insights.

### Scientific education

In spite of the lack of opportunities for work and status for young scientists in many countries, there is, nevertheless, on a worldwide basis a critical shortage both of creative scientists and of technicians to assist them. One answer is to increase the quantity and improve the quality of scientific education at all levels, but particularly in colleges and secondary schools. At present, scientific subjects are usually taught from a syllabus which is not only difficult and dull, but several decades out of date. In some schools in the United States and elsewhere successful changes in scientific teaching have been made. In these new curricula the marvelous advances of the past few decades in mathematics, physics, and chemistry are used to stretch the minds and stir the imaginations of young people, and at the same time accelerate the pace of their scientific education. Some of these new curricula are now being adapted to conditions in other countries, but the rate of utilization has lagged, in part because of the conservatism of educators and the slow pace of governments, and in part because of inadequate communication among educators. UNESCO has recognized the need for international cooperation in developing scientific education and has initiated several pilot projects to test and evaluate new methods. Literally hundreds of summer institutes for training of secondary school and college science teachers have been conducted in India by the National Science Foundation of the United States, and modern mathematical teaching at primary and secondary school levels has been initiated in ten African nations, through holding of workshops and teacher training courses and production of textbooks, under an experimental program sponsored by the Agency for International Development.

## MECHANISMS OF INTERNATIONAL SCIENTIFIC COOPERATION

The simplest and perhaps the best mechanism of international cooperation in science involves two or three scientists from different countries working together in the same laboratory on a common problem. Often one is a teacher, the others his students. But in science all are equals; ideas and insights more often than not come from the students.

Many more formal means exist, varying widely in complexity and effectiveness—generally in inverse ratio.

For many years, private scientific and philanthropic foundations have played a major role in international scientific cooperation. During the last fifteen years their activities have been overshadowed by the large-scale operations of governments, but the effectiveness of the foundations per unit of money or effort still ranks very high, because of their sophistication and experience.

The principal international organizations of scientists themselves are 15 great international unions and their co-ordinating body, the International Council of Scientific Unions (ICSU). The unions are very effective in fostering scientific communications through congresses and symposia, but they have proven singularly ineffective in cooperative research programs. Consequently, the Council has developed a new device: the special committee consisting of a small group of scientists drawn from one or more unions and operating through national committees in the cooperating countries. The International Geophysical Year and the International Indian Ocean Expedition were outstanding examples of cooperative research programs carried through or initiated by a special committee. A similar undertaking on the interactions between human beings and their biological environment, called the International Biological Program, was begun in 1967 and will continue to 1972.

The International Council is now in a critical stage, largely because of the increasing recognition by governments of the importance of international science and their consequent desire to control it. Intergovernmental scientific organizations, though largely at a remove from scientists themselves, are more and more coming to dominate the international scientific scene. ICSU can meet this challenge only by very serious attention to the planning, organization and staffing of its activities and probably also by giving a greater voice in its affairs to the national academies of member countries.

A few regional organizations of scientists such as the Pacific Science Association and the Pan Indian Ocean Association, have been successful in fostering international scientific communication, at least in certain fields. However, these organizations have been even less effective than the international unions in developing programs of cooperative research.

Several United Nations agencies have undertaken responsibilities for international scientific cooperation within their fields of cognizance. Some, such as the World Meteorological Organization, the International Atomic Energy Agency, and the Intergovernmental Oceanographic Commission, are concerned exclusively with science and technology. Others, such as UNESCO, the World Health Organization, and the Food and Agriculture Organization, have broad missions which include scientific as well as other activities. All suffer from an inadequate budget, ponderous administrative machinery, and insufficient technical staff. Nevertheless, they thoroughly justify themselves as essential components of international scientific action. If they did not already exist it would be necessary to invent them.

Some regional intergovernmental organizations, such as the International Council for the Exploration of the Sea and the European Center for Nuclear Research, have effectively advanced scientific research on an international scale. Others, such as the Organization of American States (OAS), have as yet had little impact. At Punta del Este, Uruguay, in 1967, the American chiefs of state resolved to establish a Regional Scientific and Technological Development Program to advance science and technology as a stimulus to economic development, and later in the year the Council of OAS appointed a group of scientists and engineers to study the possibilities for such a program.

### O.E.C.D. and the new international corporations

Two relatively new mechanisms for scientific and technical cooperation on a regional basis have recently arisen: the Organization for Economic Cooperation and Development (OECD), and the international corporation. The members of OECD are the industrialized countries of the market-economy world: the nations of Western and Southern Europe, the United States, Canada and Japan. The Organization is concerned with science and technology as one of the foundations of economic growth and social development, and consequently it has laid much emphasis on the formation of national science policies within its member countries—both policies for the management of science and scientific education and the allocation of resources for their support; and policies to guide and accelerate the impact of research and development on other sectors of society. In helping to formulate policies for management and support of science, it has developed a technique of objective examination of problems, trends, level and scope of effort, and methods of organization for science within a member state by a team of eminent, broadly experienced specialists from other countries. This is followed by a "confrontation" in which the examiners, together with science policy leaders from all the member countries, discuss the results of the examination and question the representatives (usually a group headed by the minister of science or an equivalent official) of the country being examined. Particular attention is paid to the balance between applied and "pure" science, the allocation of resources among different fields, plans and programs for education of scientists and technologists in the light of potential needs, communications systems for scientific and technical information, and the relevance of research efforts to national goals.

One of the ways in which OECD is attempting to increase the impact of science and technology on the welfare of its member states is through sponsoring cooperative research programs on a number of broad problems which require sustained governmental efforts but do not usually fall within the cognizance of a single government department. These include urbanism, advanced transportation technology, the management of water research, improvement of the quality of the environment, the development of new materials, and other highly complex problems which cannot be solved by a single discipline and demand contributions from scientists, engineers, economists, sociologists, political scientists, and systems analysts. Most such multi-variant subjects are not presently of much competitive commercial interest, though the solutions could give rise to great new industries.

The world oil companies are early examples of international corporations; but these have now appeared in many advanced technical fields, including pharmaceuticals, electronics, and computers, largely as a result of the aggressive and imaginative approach of American industrial managers to the opportunities offered by the European Common Market. The future possibilities for the creation of a supra-national economic structure as a result of the activities of these corporations are very promising, but they are already contributing on a large scale to cooperation across national boundaries in applied science and technology, through establishing and operating laboratories and research centers in many European countries.

## NATIONAL BARRIERS TO COOPERATION

Many kinds of national barriers interfere with the freedom and advance of science. They include economic restrictions on the passage of instruments across national boundaries; passport and visa restrictions which often involve conference-killing delays; and restrictions on the geographical areas of operation of research craft and scientific exploring parties. All these barriers involve the policies of governments, hence interactions between the scientific community in each country and its government, and between the international scientific community and the various intergovernmental organizations are needed to reduce or remove the obstacles.

### Visa and immigration barriers

During the early 1950's it was almost impossible to hold an international scientific conference in the United States because of the difficulties of getting many prominent scientists through the visa and immigration barriers.

The law prohibits the issuance of a visa on some 30 different grounds, including past or present membership in proscribed organizations or advocacy of subversive doctrines. Legally the Consular Officer on the spot has the final authority to decide whether a visa shall be issued, and his decision is not subject to any judicial or administrative review whatsoever. In principle, a scientist from one of the Iron Curtain countries would appear to be ineligible for a visa, both because he probably belongs to proscribed organizations and because he is liable to advocate subversive doctrines.

In the last several years, however, the problems of visas and immigration restrictions for foreign scientists coming to the United States have been considerably eased, not by legislation but through administrative action by the State Department and the Immigration Service. Applicants for a visa no longer need to fill out complicated and puzzling questionnaires and they are no longer fingerprinted. For most applicants, non-immigrant "visitor" visas are now issued by larger United States Consular posts in less than an hour's time on the first visit. In nearly all cases, visitors armed with a visa are passed by the Immigration Service, even though the applicant has to meet the same tests at the port of entry that he met when applying for a visa, and the Immigration Officer's determination is independent of that of the Consular Officer.

In present practice, Consular Officers refer most doubtful cases to the Departments of State and Justice, who can and usually do waive most of the grounds of ineligibility if the applicant is coming for a temporary visit. Departmental officers, by using their discretionary authority, now usually admit scientists from recognized communist countries, and the problem ordinarily resolves itself into getting the visas issued before the conference is over. Many a conference organizer has suffered a mild neurosis in his attempts to quicken the stately pace of the State Department. It is still very difficult to get scientists from certain countries through the barriers. These are the countries which the State Department does not recognize, such as mainland China, or which in its view do not exist, such as East Germany.

Until recently, it was harder to obtain admission for some scientists from non-communist countries than for scientists from the communist bloc. In May of 1967, however, the Department of State announced that group waivers could be arranged for international meetings held in the U.S., which means that visas can be issued to prospective participants living in non-communist countries even though they are, or have at one time been, members of communist organizations and would normally be excluded by law. The Allied Travel Office in Berlin, has decided that an East German scientist who is also a government or party official can now receive a visa for a professional visit to a NATO country on the understanding he will not use his visit for political activity. It has also become possible for American physicians, scientists and other scholars to have their passports validated for professional visits to Albania, mainland China, Cuba, North Korea and North Vietnam.

### *Removal of barriers by intergovernmental action*

Two examples of intergovernmental actions to facilitate scientific research are the Treaty on Antarctica and the International Convention on the Scientific Exploration of the Continental Shelf. In the Antarctic Treaty the entire continent was set aside as a theatre for scientific research and exploration, and all the signatory countries agreed to waive any claims to Antarctic territory for the next 50 years. The Convention on the Continental Shelf provides that scientific research in the shallow coastal areas outside territorial waters can be conducted by scientists of any country, provided the research culminates in open publication and scientists from the coastal state are allowed to participate. The coastal state must give its permission for such research, but the Convention provides that "this permission will not ordinarily be refused."

The commerical preemption of radio frequencies for television and communications is a potential barrier to research in radio-astronomy, space science, oceanography, and meteorology. The International Council of Scientific Unions, greatly aided by UNESCO and the World Meteorological Organization has taken vigorous and successful steps to obtain allocations from the International Telecommunications Union of critically important frequencies for radio-astronomy, and for communications from anchored bouys used in oceanography and meteorology.

### INTELLECTUAL BARRIERS

Far-reaching advances in science have usually come from individual scientists or groups of scientists doing what they are interested in at the moment, freely and excitedly following up new observations or insights in an essentially anarchic and unplanned fashion. The cumbersome apparatus of planning, logistics, agreement, and direction essential for cooperative international research is repellent to this kind of science.

In general the planning and direction of international scientific action is done either by bureaucrats or by so-called scientific statesmen, usually men who have long since ceased to do significant scientific research. Science is a young man's game, and the young giants who are the real creators need to be brought in. But often they are too busy with their own research to be bothered with how other people should do theirs. Science has become so expensive and so important that it can only be supported financially by governments, but there is still in all countries, even the most advanced ones, a lack of understanding by politicians of science as a human activity, a situation often matched by the equally profound misunderstanding of politics by scientists. Governments are usually interested only in the applicable results of science, which they regard as a tool: one among many to be used in the accomplishment of social, economic, foreign policy, or military objectives, and one that is effective only over a fairly long time. Consequently, they do not hesitate to restrict or impede scientific activity to serve short-range goals. The concept of science for its own sake of gaining understanding—because understanding is a natural right of human beings—has never been more than partially accepted by politicians. Under these circumstances, progress toward a true international free-masonry of science must necessarily be slow.

### SOME EXAMPLES OF EARTH-WIDE PROGRAMS

#### *The International Geophysical Year*

By far the largest, most complex, and most expensive enterprise ever undertaken in international scientific cooperation was the International Geophysical Year. The IGY involved about 60,000 scientists and technicians from 66 nations working at thousands of stations literally from pole to pole. No one has ventured to estimate the total cost, but it was certainly in excess of a billion dollars. This vast and daring enterprise caught the imagination of the world and gave men everywhere a new conception of their planetary home. It helped to construct scientific bridges across political chasms, and greatly increased the role of science and of scientists in national policy-making and in diplomacy. Much solid scientific accomplishment also came out of the IGY.

The joint assault on Antarctica by some thirteen nations gave us a new level of knowledge about the shape and topography of that ice-buried continent. Coordinated studies of particles from the sun and their effects on the earth's upper atmosphere and surrounding plasma were made possible by the elaborate planning and communications systems developed during the IGY. New impetus was given to seismology and the study of the earth's interior. In oceanography, much was learned about the ocean currents deep beneath the surface of the sea, and about the shape and structure of the deep sea floor. The great adventure of our time, man's exploration of outer space, began during the IGY, and was undoubtedly accelerated by it.

But perhaps of equal importance for the future was the IGY discovery of a most effective means of international scientific cooperation. Nearly all the money spent during the IGY was used by each nation separately in support of its own scientists who were taking part in the international program. Only a few hundred thousand dollars were required for the apparatus of international coordination. Committees of scientists in each participating country developed their own programs, and these were presented to scientists of the other countries in a series of international meetings where plans for extensive modifications—usually expansions—were made. Scientists of each country would then return home and put pressure on their government to provide financial support for the national program developed in the conference, basing their arguments largely on "keeping up with the Joneses." Thus the great enterprise grew by a series of bootstrap-lifting stages.

Another long-range benefit of the IGY was its development of mechanisms for exchange of scientific data. World data centers were established in the United States, the U.S.S.R., and in Europe, and elaborate agreements were entered into by the scientists of the participating countries to provide each of these centers with all of the measurements made under the different scientific programs. As far as is known, these agreements were fairly well kept.

The peculiar virtues of the IGY centered on avoidance of a ponderous international bureaucracy; planning in each country by the scientists directly involved—an arrangment which led to a liberal interpretation of the objectives and scope of the scientific work eligible for support under the IGY umbrella; development of a means for large-scale support by individual governments; and development of mechanisms for free exchange of a wide variety of scientific data.

But the IGY had defects as well as virtues: the emphasis was inevitably on systematic collection of relatively routine observations rather than on the individual theoretical and experimental work which constitutes the chief means of progress in scientific understanding. The whole enterprise was a high-pressure affair, and consequently its cost, in terms of human effort, as well as money, was perhaps excessive relative to the results obtained. Political considerations intruded themselves to the extent that the great land mass of mainland China was blanked out in the international program of observations. At least in certain fields, the scientific representatives of some countries at the international planning conferences had no real authority to agree to any modifications of their national programs. Hence, there was far less coordination of the actual scientific work than would have been desirable.

### Cooperation in Outer Space

The United Nations Treaty on Outer Space, beside prohibiting the use of nuclear weapons in space, calls both for a regime of law in human space activities and for scientific cooperation and exchange of results obtained in astrophysical and geophysical research. Under the terms of the Treaty, outer space and celestial bodies, like the high seas and Antarctica, are free for exploration by all states in conformity with international law, and are not subject to appropriation.

At present, the deep political differences of our time place an upper limit on space cooperation. Soviet and American astronauts will probably not ride to the moon on the same space ship. But there is, or should be, also a lower limit to this cooperation, if the nations can take a realistic view of their own self-interests. All countries, whatever their ideology, can agree that cooperative experiments should be undertaken and information exchanged, and that the potentialities of earth satellites for improving worldwide weather services and communications among nations should be developed.

The Committee on Space Research of the International

Council of Scientific Unions serves as a common meeting ground for American and Soviet space scientists, as well as for those of other nationalities. On a bilateral basis, the National Aeronautics and Space Administration has cooperative ventures with some forty countries, involving tracking stations, exchanges of personnel, and joint space experiments. The United States also helps the European Space Research Organization and its member countries by launching their space vehicles.

An international sounding rocket facility has been constructed in south India to facilitate experiments with scientific rockets near the equator. This launching base will be of great value in exploring the peculiar phenomena of the high upper atmosphere that exist in the neighborhood of the equator, and in some unknown way are related to the rotation of the earth.

### Weather forecasting and research

Orbiting weather satellites, supplementing other advances in meteorological technology, such as sounding rockets, radar, electronic computers, and instrumented ocean buoys have made it possible for the first time to observe the entire atmosphere of the earth continuously in time and from a fairly close grid of points in space, and to handle the data obtained in a usefully short time. To exploit these new capabilities, the World Meteorological Organization (WMO) is developing an international weather service. This is based on a global network, called the World Weather Watch, to obtain and use meteorological information from weather satellites as well as from land-based instruments and from weather ships and anchored buoys on the high seas. Three world weather centers for collection, processing, and dissemination of these data have been established in Washington, Moscow, and Melbourne. Regional centers are being organized, and gaps in the world grid of land and ocean observatories, which has been very thin in the Southern Hemisphere, are being filled. The United States is making available to other countries through this program the information obtained from its weather satellites, and it is hoped that the Soviet Union will soon develop and disseminate information from its own system.

In the long run, international cooperation in meteorological research may be more important than this development of meteorological services. To explore these possibilities, a collaborative effort, the Global Atmospheric Research Program, is being organized between the World Meteorological Organization and the community of atmospheric scientists, operating through the International Council of Scientific Unions. In the words of a recent WMO report, "It is not unrealistic to expect that mankind will eventually have the power to influence weather and even climate on a large scale." By encouraging cooperation now, we may reduce the risk that this power will eventually be used by one nation to achieve military or economic advantage at the expense of others.

### The International Biological Program (IBP)

This five-year Program, in which scientists of some 40 nations are participating, has three related objectives: human welfare, scientific advance and the development of international scientific cooperation. These three objectives cannot be separated. Biologists can contribute uniquely to human welfare only by advancing scientific understanding, and the basic premise of the IBP is that the growth of understanding will be accelerated by international cooperation among the world's biologists.

The research being undertaken in the IBP aims at the development of scientific ecology in its broadest sense, with special emphasis on the genetics and dynamics of populations; the factors that control biological productivity; the ways in which plants and animals, and especially men, adapt to their environment; and the changing distribution of living things in the sea and the air, and on the land.

New research methods are being developed and old ones greatly extended. In the past, ecologists have studied particular limited communities; now, work on a few large-scale systems is being conducted to test and extend our understanding. New approaches to worldwide biological surveys are being introduced to improve the level of description of the biosphere.

The underlying concept of the IBP is the belief of many biologists that too little is understood about the complex interrelationships among living things to be able to predict the effects of technical change, or to help the technologists in conserving the values and utilizing the abundance of the world of life. They believe greater understanding will make it possible for man to respond to opportunity as well as to react to need.

## THE FEDERAL GOVERNMENT AND INTERNATIONAL SCIENCE

The importance of the scientific health of the country, the relationship between science and national strength and security, and the increasing costs of research have led to general acceptance of the idea that financial support for science in the United States is a necessary function of the federal government.

As the government has expanded its involvement, it has found itself engaged to an ever-increasing extent in international scientific activities. It has sponsored international scientific expeditions, enabled American scientists to participate in international conferences and helped support their international organizations, brought foreign scientists to the United States, cooperated with other nations in mounting experiments, and given financial assistance to foreign research workers and laboratories.

In accordance with the historical pattern of development of United States government activities, federal scientific involvement overseas has grown in a haphazard fashion through the action of individual agencies which have seen a need in the light of their own missions. As the picture has emerged, however, we can now see that the government's participation in international scientific activities has been chiefly rooted in three principles:

1. To advance science and technology in the United States, it is desirable to encourage wide contacts between American and foreign scientists, engage in international scientific ventures, and support some scientists of other countries in their research;

2. To maintain our military security, a strong scientific establishment must be built in allied countries, scientific competence must be utilized wherever it is available; and there must be a rapid flow of sophisticated information about new discoveries and innovations made outside the United States.

3. The advancement of science in all nations contributes to man's intellectual and material well-being, and hence aids in achieving the long-term goals of the United States.

### United States support of research by foreign scientists

One of the international aspects of the federal involvement in science is support of the research of foreign scientists overseas. This support grew steadily from its beginning in Europe by the American military following World War II until about 1963, when the problem of the unfavorable balance of payments began to become acute; in fiscal year 1962 it was on the order of $25–30 million. Active programs are conducted by eight government departments and independent agencies.

The bulk of this support has been justified as being necessary, or at least useful, in the light of departmental or agency missions. Most agencies, when providing support, have selected foreign scientists who have some special capabilities in terms of location, competence, or facilities. The Department of Defense modifies this "uniqueness" criterion. It claims that the military interests of the United States are served by broadening their scientific base and encouraging the flow of ideas that results from close relationships with good scientists wherever they may be located.

In the less-advanced countries, we have supported research in order to assist development, as well as for its own sake. Here, the numbers of capable scientists and the help they receive from their own governments are much smaller than in the advanced countries. As a result, United States assistance to individual institutions or scientists has a far-reaching impact on the scientific life of the country.

In some of the poor countries, foreign currency surpluses earned through the sale of United States agricultural commodities (PL–480 Funds) are used to finance research. Apparently as an accident of administrative agreement, the support of research is given a lower priority than other uses to which the PL–480 funds may be put. The result is that local currency is available for research only when all other needs have been satisfied. The funds in local currency are often usefully salted with small amounts of dollar funds for purchase of equipment and scientific journals, and for travel.

Concentration on supporting research overseas related to the missions of United States agencies leaves many gaps where, for a mixture of scientific and foreign policy purposes, the United States government should be active. Support related to foreign aid can be budgeted through the Agency for International Development, but there are other situations where technical assistance is not involved and the research program is not strictly within agency missions, yet should be supported. To meet this need, the National Science Foundation, as the only federal agency charged with looking after the health of United States science as a whole, supports each year 20 or 30 projects abroad in the grey area of mixed scientific and foreign policy objectives.

Other agencies, such as Agriculture, Health, Education and Welfare, and Interior, that are working in fields directly related to human welfare, should also be given limited responsibility to support basic research that furthers their fields of emphasis, whether or not the practical application of the research is tied to a problem encountered in the United States. Particularly in the PL–480 program the restriction of pertinency to a United States domestic problem could be removed without raising fiscal difficulties.

In the early days of United States support of research in Europe, our programs were an important factor in many countries in increasing their awareness of the values and usefulness of science, thereby helping to raise the level of domestic support provided for research. In some nations these programs helped to keep good scientists productive, and prevented frustration during a period when the national government was unable to provide full support itself. Our assistance encouraged scientists to remain as residents of their native lands, rather than migrate to the United States or elsewhere. Scientists working on United States grants or contracts were able to visit the United States and thereby to increase face-to-face scientific communication. American support aided in identfying promising younger scientists, and enabled outstanding university teachers to take responsibility for more graduate students. These programs also demonstrated that governments can support science across national borders effectively, and, to a measure, disinterestedly for the good of all men and nations. The patterns thus begun may prove to be of great and lasting value.

The rapidly advancing economic situation in the developed countries should now lead us in a different direction—to emphasis on cooperative research. Cooperation can be multilateral or bilateral, but it should involve investment by all parties concerned. Scientists from other countries should be encouraged to plan a project jointly with American scientists and to submit a joint proposal to both governments. Such bilateral cooperation between American and Japanese scientists in several different fields began in the early 1960's, sponsored jointly in this country by the State Department and the National Science Foundation; a similar arrangement has recently been entered into with Italy. The National Aeronautics and Space Administration in its overseas programs has insisted on local support for cooperative projects.

Joint planning and submission of proposals does not happen automatically; the research-supporting agencies need actively to encourage such planning and to provide support for necessary travel and meetings.

### SCIENCE AND FOREIGN POLICY

In the past, international scientific cooperation has been most successful when it has dealt with the problems of communication among scientists, with removal of the barriers to scientific research, or with other matters regarding what might be called the internal business of science.

But scientific and technological developments can and often do have profound effects on economic and social change and the relative power of nations, and consequently on the environment within which foreign policy is formulated. The development and spread of nuclear weapons technology, the emergence of economically competitive nuclear power, the rapid development of the computer and of solid-state electronics industries, satellite communications, modern agricultural research, the evolution of new techniques for surveying, analyzing and developing resources, and the emergence of new technologies which can significantly affect the growth of human populations are simply a few examples of scientific results which have an important relation to United States objectives in other sectors of our international relations.

Yet only the beginnings of the necessary mechanisms

exist within the State Department for establishing a foreign policy for science or for integrating scientific factors into other aspects of foreign policy formulation.

One reason for this deficiency may be a feeling among the leaders of the Department that the changes brought about by these developments will be slow to take effect and can be brought into account as they emerge by conventional diplomatic means. They may well be right about this.

But the same cannot be said of the Department's consistent failure to recognize the immediate cultural values of American science for our relations with other countries. Science in both its aspects is a form of art, and one in which the United States now leads the world. By encouraging and promoting the widest possible range of international activities for American science, the Department could greatly foster acceptance of the Western intellectual tradition, improve relationships with intellectual groups in the communist world, help develop common goals and objectives both with the rich and the poor nations, strengthen international organizations, and enhance the image of the United States as a nation concerned with more than material things.

A few years ago the Department announced, with considerable fanfare, the creation of a new Office of International Scientific Affairs, whose Director would be a Principal Officer of the Department with rank administratively equivalent to a Bureau head. The functions of the Office were expanded to include cognizance of the peaceful uses of outer space and atomic energy, which had previously been handled separately. Among his other functions, the Director was to participate actively in general foreign policy development, ensuring that appropriate consideration was given to scientific and technological factors; and to advise and assist the Secretary of State in reaching decisions on matters having scientific and technological implications.

Experience has shown that the holder of this position has no real authority and little influence, and is effectively isolated from the centers of power in the Department. The first Director of the New Office was a widely respected physicist. But he resigned in 1963 and was succeeded by an acting Director, a career Foreign Service Officer with no scientific training or experience. The Office is still functioning without a scientifically trained head, apparently because no scientist of the requisite qualifications has been found who would take the job.

A more effective mechanism is also required overseas to provide and evaluate information on the situation of science and technology in each country, recommend policy and program changes, and implement policy decisions. This could be accomplished through strengthening and expanding the existing science attaché program, particularly in those countries or regions in which the United States has extensive scientific interests. At present there are 25 overseas posts for Science Attachés in 16 countries, plus OECD, but five of these posts are vacant.

The science attaché program might be considerably improved if it were operated jointly by the State Department and the National Science Foundation. Just as the military and agricultural attachés are the joint responsibility of the Departments of Defense and Agriculture, respectively, the Foundation could provide both guidance for the program and personnel for service as Science Attachés.

# 5. Beyond the Present

## KENNETH W. THOMPSON

The temptation for those caught up in the turbulence of the struggle to survive is to view the world through harsh headlines and the clash of contending ideologies and conflicting social movements. Viewed from this vantage point, man's stake in the prospects for the future is "poor, nasty, brutish and short." He can anticipate little more than a monotonous round of conflicts that at best can be contained and ameliorated. Nations and groups replace one another in contention, but the struggle goes on and any hope for an early harmony of interests appears distant and utopian. The future for peace, progress and justice is no brighter today than in the past.

Fortunately, this picture of the world may be more apparent than real. It rests on the projection of visible and well-publicized forces that daily commentators can isolate and assess and that catch the eye of busy readers who supposedly prefer simplification and sensationalism. Waves crashing against the shore are more readily described than deep running currents. We see that part of the iceberg jutting out from the water but are neither predisposed nor helped to perceive the greater mass hidden beneath the surface. Yet this portion of reality is the more substantial and enduring.

The sources of the world's common cultural and scientific heritage take root both in tradition and present reality. Historically, social mobility and the intersection of trends of thought and practice have knit the world together more profoundly than is commonly acknowledged. Even the occasional traveller in Africa is soon aware of the overlay of British, French, European and American customs and ideas. Present day indigenous cultures are a blending of ancient tribal patterns and modern western practices. Science, which is a precondition of modernization, has brought with it certain assumptions about man, social organization, predictability and human betterment that owe their validity to the experiences of Western civilization. The diffusion of culture has made national societies a melting pot and what is common to many cultures is as real as what is unique to each.

Beyond this, present reality has put a premium on the emergence of national goals and purposes that are much the same in rich and poor, developed and underdeveloped societies. It has not always been so. For much of the world only a few decades ago, poverty, ignorance and subservience were accepted as foreordained. Life for the masses from birth to death was a treadmill of suffering and deprivation interrupted only by the simple rewards inherent in primitive and pastoral life. Today all around the world, voices are raised in a single chorus. The revolution of rising expectations, however premature and over-sanguine, leads men to ask: "Who would not rather be fed than hungry, educated than ignorant, free than enslaved, housed than destitute, masters in their own house, not servants in more spacious mansions?" The chorus has not reached its crescendo; the plans for realizing these goals are often vague and unformed. It is no exaggeration to say that mankind is on the march toward a way of life that others have achieved in the sight and memory of the living. Having shared a common literary and philosophical heritage with the West, the developing societies today aspire to the institutions and privileges from which their adopted tradition stems.

It is at this point that cultural affairs have increasingly become part of international relations. Given the aspirations and claims of emerging societies, the developed nations have no choice but to join in educational and scientific relations as they once engaged primarily in diplomatic and military relations. This trend is bound to grow in scope and character in the future. Present malaise and temporary resistance to providing the wherewithal can delay but not eliminate it. Forces are at work in the world that are more important than success or failure of present programs or endeavors. Moreover, the imperative to join in the common effort knows no ideological or geographic bounds. Communist states, for the same mixture of policies and motives as democratic nations, are constrained to help. Moreover, there are hopeful signs that once disadvantaged societies which have attained some measure of progress are rising to the challenge of assisting their neighbors. Fifteen years ago, Mexico, which was just beginning to remedy its crop deficit problem was reluctant to share new varieties of corn and wheat with Central American countries. Today the International Corn and Wheat Center in Mexico has become a clearing house for crop materials that are welcome not only in Mexico but around the world. Pakistan and India have greater optimism about the future partly because through the use and adaptation of large quantities of Mexican wheat they can look forward to greatly increased yields. This pattern is being duplicated in other areas and disciplines throughout the world.

The central question for countries like the United States is what can we draw from the past and present in guiding us in the future? What lessons have we learned from past cultural relations? How shall we draw our priorities, and who can help us in this task? What are appropriately the concerns of national programs and where must the focus, as Senator William Fulbright has argued, be on multilateral and international efforts?

The nub of our problem is that cultural programs, as critics of UNESCO argue, rapidly proliferate and there can be a certain lack of cohesiveness that binds together the many worthwhile endeavors that make up the cultural enterprise. To the extent culture is conceived of as part of American foreign policy—and not all American efforts, whether public or private, fall within this framework—it is subject to the same constraints that govern other actions. Those who project worthwhile endeavors must range them in some hierarchical order. They must separate vital and essential efforts from those that, however worthy, are less critically needed. Where funding is concerned, they must distinguish between activities of first priority and those of second or third order importance. In no area is this more painful and difficult than the cultural realm.

GUIDES TO THE FUTURE

*Institution building*

Institution building has taken on major importance because of growing recognition that what is left behind is even more significant than what is done *ad interim,* especially in developing countries. This is dramatically true with cultural exchange. International exchange is undergoing a basic and far-reaching reappraisal in major western countries. The fact is that thorough studies and fundamental inquiries on which to base conclusions are lacking. There is need for "a Conant study" of international student exchange. We have impressions but little hard data on the effects of mass student exchange programs—for example, of Chinese students in the 1920's and 1930's. For the present, therefore, impressions take the place of solidly grounded conclusions. So long as these sharply drawn and perhaps exaggerated impressions prevail, the quality and significance of large-scale and sometimes indiscriminate exchanges remains in doubt. For the impression is widespread of the rootless, de-nationalized and de-tribalized student alienated from the folkways and customs of his people, made accustomed to social and scientific affluence, disoriented by preoccupation with techniques and concerns with little relevance to his own society, and progressively drawn apart from genuine service to his community and nation. Partly in reaction to this situation, a new pattern of international education is emerging. Its stage is the home country of the foreign student, not the United States. The actors, as in the past, are masses of students and numbers of professors and young instructors joined in a common endeavor. Their purpose is better education more closely linked to the needs of an indigenous people. Their movement is reversed, for whereas in the earliest phase of international exchange, hundreds and thousands of foreign students journeyed to the United States, now tens of thousands of American professors are taking up residence in foreign institutions around the world. Their task remains that of educating foreign students not in an American but in their own cultural setting. As partners, not observers, Americans have joined national and expatriate educators in institution building within another social and political context. They become part of the fabric of a society which has the power to use or misuse, assimilate or isolate, welcome or reject the graduates of the newly emerging educational process. They live and labor on the front line of an educational system evolving to meet local needs and prepare leaders for national responsibilities. They exchange the role of American critics standing in judgment on other educational systems for that of participants in social and educational invention seeking to blend and adapt separate but compatible traditions of learning. If the education they provide is irrelevant to society's needs, they must share responsibility.

The consequences that flow from the new pattern of international exchange call for review and analysis. First, the primary target of intellectual cooperation has shifted. It has become, in the first instance, institution building. The lesson of a century of experience in the business of international exchange is that educating individuals is not enough. Every private and public agency has its warehouse of files recounting the melancholy experiences of individuals whose intellectual formation abroad left little to be desired but who, on returning, found scant outlet for their talents. Where the appropriate educational and scientific framework was missing, writers became clerks, economists became bank tellers and scientists became salesmen. Coffee shops in the Middle East and Africa abound with economically displaced lawyers, accountants and teachers. A much quoted slogan for talent hunters has been, "Find the bright and promising individual for study abroad and the future will take care of itself." Like many slogans, this guideline is too simple and less than half the story.

Responsibility for the selection of fellows and scholars for study in the United States is not easily or rapidly discharged. Choice is always a serious and awesome task. Some ivory hunters are more successful than others in identifying excellence, as the records of men like Henry Allen Moe of the Guggenheim Foundation and the late Walter Rogers of the Institute of Current World Affairs make plain. John D. Rockefeller, 3rd, Chairman of the Board of The Rockefeller Foundation, periodically reminds officers that since only a few are chosen, recipients of Foundation fellowships should be judged both as scholars and as prospective leaders in their fields. Moreover, responsibility is not discharged through the identification of excellence alone. Especially in the developing countries, the question must be asked: What are the chances of a well-trained man pursuing his subject? Some countries need general practitioners and para-medical personnel but only a few are ready for specialists in open heart surgery. Is it sensible for grant-making agencies to submerge the scholarly community of a country in educational opportunities unreleated to its most pressing needs?

When people identify persistent needs which must be met through efforts either by the private or public sector, institutions spring up to provide organized ways of coping with problems. Modernization in democratic and non-democratic systems alike has brought with it large-scale social aggregation. Mass societies tend to create administrative units in which arbitrary choices are subordinated to routine procedures and tables of organizations. Education is no exception to this trend toward bureaucratization. Hopefully societies retain flexibility in the operation of large-scale organizations, but the outside agency which would assist must for the most part work within them. Moreover, trained personnel must find their place in the social organizations of a particular country and those who would foster further training are obliged to know as much about institutions as about individuals. It is as irresponsible to appraise individuals and not the institutions in which they must work as to consider institutions and disregard the quality of individuals.

The most successful fellowship programs of private foundations have been those in which trained manpower has, at the termination of a period of study abroad, found an institutional home. Particularly noteworthy are the fellowships awarded by The Rockefeller Foundation for agriculture in Mexico. Scores of young Mexicans trained in leading American schools of agriculture have returned to responsible positions in the Ministry of Agriculture or in institutions such as the Graduate School at Chapingo. Similarly, European social scientists on leave from national institutions of higher learning while studying in graduate centers in the United States

today occupy a high proportion of social science professor-
ships on the continent. The experience of medical and natural scientists from Europe and Latin America chosen for
Rockefeller Foundation fellowships is another case in point.
In 1960, Foundation officers reviewing a representative sam-
ple of a thousand fellows discovered that all but one had
returned to their native countries—a tribute to the careful
screening, strict requirement of an institutional affiliation at
the time of interview, and repeated discussions with institutional leadership. This record drawn from the history of one
foundation reflects a common experience of those who administer fellowships. The evidence is clear that there is no
substitute for rigorous and systematic procedures giving
equal attention to both sides of the equation, namely, the
individual and his institution.

A second consequence resulting from the changing patterns of international exchange is to shift to an emphasis on
graduate education for foreign students. Nothing could be
more self-defeating than an approach to intellectual cooperation that coupled institution building in developing countries with exchanges that drained local institutions of the
flower of the undergraduate student population. Yet to a
considerable extent, American agencies find themselves
working at cross purposes in countries with fledgling institutions of higher education. For example officials of the newly
federated University of East Africa complain that places in
their colleges are going unfilled at a time when undergraduate fellowships are multiplying for study in the United
States. The facts are in dispute and the truth hard to come
by; it is argued that many young Africans admitted for study
in American institutions cannot gain admission to African
universities because of the stringency of educational requirements. To deny them the opportunity to study in American
institutions is to deny them a college education.

Few dispute the fact, however, that generally speaking a
solid undergraduate degree from a recognized institution in
the student's native country carries advantages. It enables
him to study with those who must furnish his country's
leadership. Ties of mutual respect and national self-con-
sciousness form around a common educational experience.
A greater awareness of the nation's problems and its hu-

man resources develops in its own classrooms and on its playing fields. The curriculum is more likely to be relevant and education more likely to extend into local communities to meet pressing needs. Finally, an institution with sufficient prestige to train its native sons is on the way to earning the right to serve the economy and the state.

If institution building in developing countries leads to a certain de-emphasis on undergraduate training abroad, the opposite is true of graduate programs. Professional schools more likely than not lack resources. With the explosion of knowledge and the growing complexity of advanced subject matter in major fields, it is asking too much of infant universities that they simultaneously mount undergraduate and graduate programs. Even older new universities such as the University of the Philippines will probably limit themselves to M.A. level courses at least in the foreseeable future. Faculty development must precede the launching of across the board graduate training even though the pressures for building a complete university will doubtless increase.

Notwithstanding, opportunities for graduate study in the United States for educational leaders from developing countries should be maintained and increased. For some, admission to the best graduate centers is immediately appropriate and attainable. Others may find their place in hand-tailored M.A. curricula such as the Institute for Economic Development at Williams College. Still others may require an intermediate year of intensive study in an outstanding liberal arts college. Latin American students slated for medical school have profited greatly from a year of advanced undergraduate study in the basic sciences offered by Tulane University. The common theme underlying the study plans of foreign students across this broad spectrum is the quest for advanced learning or higher degrees. It seems likely that the United States will be called upon for more rather than less assistance in the realm of graduate and professional study.

A third consequence that stems from the new form of international exchange relates to the role of visiting American faculty and administrative assistance to the developing university. If the flow of masses of undergraduates to

American universities is to be replaced by the movement of outstanding American educators to the new universities, considerable inventiveness and experimentation is called for. Most American scholars are not accustomed to a period of service abroad. Until fairly recently expatriate scholars were predominantly British scientists and professors serving abroad. Ironically, the demand for Americans occurs concurrently with rising pressures and expanding enrollments on the American scene. Britain, with a long tradition of international service, is caught up in staffing the new universities in England. It remains true that Britain has gone further in building up cadres of career servants willing and able to operate on foreign soil. For example, the British Council can field a permanent team of 120 English language teachers for overseas missions whereas the United States must depend on term or contract personnel.

As public programs, particularly those financed by the Agency for International Development, have multiplied, the help of American universities has been enlisted. AID has undertaken to forge a partnership in technical assistance between itself, universities and developing institutions. A recent report observes: "As of December 31, 1963, 72 universities in the United States were performing technical assistance tasks under 129 separate contracts with AID. More than $158 million was involved in these contracts."[1] Today AID is involved in the support of more than eighty universities abroad. Collaboration by American universities in public programs is nothing new under the sun, for present relationships overseas are merely an extension of earlier collaboration in such fields as national defense and agriculture. Universities have much to gain for science, scholarship knows no national boundaries, and tomorrow's student must obtain a grasp of other cultures.

However, the common interests of AID and the universities in the outside world have not prevented frictions and misunderstandings, reviewed in detail in the Gardner Report. Partly this results from the long-term nature of the task. To paraphrase Woodrow Wilson, education like poli-

1. John W. Gardner, *AID and the Universities: A Report to the Administrator of the Agency for International Development,* Education and World Affairs, New York, 1964, p. 1.

tics is the "slow boring of hard wood." Short-term contracts are not always productive of long-term results. In institution building, three years should be viewed as a beginning and not the probable termination of assistance. Someone has said that American foreign aid too often has involved responding to a twenty year need with a three year program, two year personnel and one year appropriations. Universities are reluctant to undertake serious commitments when the means are not in sight of seeing the task to completion. In John Gardner's words: "The universities say that AID lags far behind other agencies, such as the National Science Foundation . . . in its understanding of universities."[2] "AID responds that the universities make no attempt to understand its problems . . . universities have often acted irresponsibly—sending third-rate personnel overseas, neglecting the needs of the host country while they concentrate on what they want to do . . . failing to put the full weight and resources of the university behind a contract, and so on."[3]

From universities, a common complaint often repeated is that AID does little to strengthen their capabilities to work abroad. AID officials respond that in the competition for scarce dollars greater urgency attaches to aiding developing countries directly. Critics of AID policies reply that viewing assistance to American institutions as competitive with aid to foreign centers is short-sighted for "if the medical profession had insisted that every dollar spent in strengthening modern medical education, technology and science was a dollar unjustly diverted from the care of patients, we would still be treating fevers with leeches."[4] This comparison may beg the question, however, for the real issue is how and where assistance to universities should be channeled. Is it general support that universities require, or aid to area studies programs, or assistance to certain basic disciplines in the arts and sciences? It may be significant that for some universities in their efforts overseas strong departments in the basic sciences and social sciences play a more creative role in institution building than area studies

2. *Ibid.*, p. 4.
3. *Ibid.*, p. 5.
4. *Ibid.*, p. 12.

centers which may be exclusively research-oriented. It remains true that other governmental agencies, notably the NSF and NIH, have found ways of helping campus-based activities as related to overseas programs.

From the standpoint of effective assistance, the selection process in identifying American universities capable of contributing abroad is basic to all that follows. Authorities point to certain problems that hinder wise choices. On the one hand, certain universities may be overly aggressive in piling contract upon contract beyond their ability to perform. On the other hand, those who make selections may be unfamiliar with universities in general or with strengths and weaknesses in particular fields. University men should appraise university potential. The quality of institutions and individuals who joined overseas in the work of the International Health Division and the Agricultural Operating Programs of The Rockefeller Foundation was a product of a simple selection formula. Basically, professionals were given the task of evaluating professionals. No scheme for clearing house or consortium operations nor the multiplying of detailed criteria can remove the importance of this simple rule. The test must be the professional competence of those who choose, and first-hand acquaintance with emergent needs in the developing institutions.

Controversy and disagreement has been greatest in the area of so-called university contracts. An extraordinarily attractive and seemingly logical principle of associating an American university with a developing one through a so-called sister university contract has provoked widespread criticism and conflict. In John Gardner's words: "Universities accuse AID of undue rigidity, incomprehensible delays, unsympathetic attitudes, and excessive and costly emphasis on small details. AID points out that universities have at times behaved irresponsibly and with little recognition of the requirements of accountability under which a government agency must function."[5]

Undoubtedly, much can be done to ease the possibility of conflict. The parties to the contract should strive for a more complete understanding of the purposes of the joint

5. *Ibid.*, p. 24.

enterprise and the responsibilities each assumes in the contract. Preliminary discussions can resolve points of difference and visits by university people to the field may clear away false impressions. University leaders from the two centers should take part in the negotiations and leaders with authority to make commitments must be signatories to the contract. Working scholars should be present at the take-off, particularly if a crash landing is to be avoided. The anatomy of successful university contracts deserves study and analysis and, as a starter, AID officials could do worse than to review the elements that contributed to the effective working relations and substantial success of partnerships such as the one between the University of Chicago and Catholic University of Chile in economics. Clearly the pivotal role of Professor Theodore Schultz in negotiation and leadership was a decisive factor. So perhaps was the focus on an identifiable and manageable discipline and the participation of first-class scholars. The teamwork between AID and the two universities was also crucial.

In recent times a new note has been sounded. Legislation has been introduced by President Johnson. This legislation is incorporated in the International Education Act of 1966. Friends of the Administration point to the bill as the first attempt to look at international education as a coherent whole. It is said that in time "it will probably be clear that a breakthrough of major proportions has been achieved."[6] The Administration bill introduced in the House by Congressmen Powell and Brademas and the Senate by Senator Morse gives form to some of the themes proclaimed by the President in an Address at the bicentennial ceremony of the Smithsonian Institution.

Three elements in the broad framework the President projects have been given special mention. First, his message offers educational cooperation to all the nations of the world, whether friend or foe. Second, he links international education to the national interest and the achievement of peace in the world. Third, by stating "We expect to receive as much as we give, to learn as well as to teach," the Presi-

6. "International Education Program, 1966," Education and World Affairs, New York, 1966.

dent underscores the reciprocal nature of education. Within the broad framework of his "grand design," the President includes more specific proposals. He calls for the establishment of a corps of education officers to serve in Embassies abroad giving focus to educational programs. Through the Department of Health, Education and Welfare, moreover, funds would be provided to colleges and universities both for the further strengthening of advanced centers in international studies and the building up of new curricula in smaller institutions. Simultaneously, assistance will be made available for improving the curriculum in world affairs in elementary and secondary schools. The focal point for leadership in the whole broad area will be the proposed Center for Educational Cooperation within HEW. AID will presumably continue its educational activities as part of country development programming in a specific and declining number of nations. The new Center's mandate neither begins nor ends at the water's edge. Its concern will be both with domestic and overseas activities aimed at long-term educational goals. It will therefore fall within its power to offer new and more promising forms of assistance to developing institutions through partnership with American universities. Yet even those who see in the new International Education Program "a breakthrough of major proportions" are frank to say that "among the items which received little explicit attention" was: "the serious manpower problem that affects the entire area of international education. Where will the people come from—and how will new recruits be found and trained—to staff all the positions here and abroad. . . ."[7] Nor does the legislation pay attention to "the need to base our international educational efforts increasingly on full collaboration with educators, scholars and other leaders of the host countries. . . ."[8] It also leaves to the future "the much discussed and ever mounting foreign student problem . . . and the urgent necessity of providing better means . . . [of] evaluating, screening and selecting them for admission to U.S. institutions."[9]

Yet an important beginning has been made to bring

7. *Ibid.*, pp. 15–16.
8. *Ibid.*, p. 16.
9. *Ibid.*, p. 16.

focus and direction into the international education field. It is of course far too early even to predict its effects on the patterns of education in the future.

### Scientific centers

The impetus for scientific cooperation is as strong or stronger than the pressures for creating indigenous institutions in the wider educational field. Writing in 1944, in his Annual Report, President Raymond B. Fosdick of the Rockefeller Foundation observed that in World War II, "an American soldier wounded on a battlefield in the Far East owes his life to the Japanese scientist, Kitasato, who isolated the bacillus of tetanus. A Russian soldier saved by a blood transfusion is indebted to Landsteiner, an Austrian. A German soldier is sheltered from typhoid fever with the help of a Russian, Metchnikoff. A Dutch marine in the East Indies is protected from malaria because of the experiments of an Italian, Grassi; . . . a British aviator in North Africa escapes death from surgical infection because a Frenchman, Pasteur, and a German, Koch, elaborated a new technique. In peace as in war we are all of us beneficiaries of contributions to knowledge made by every nation in the world. Our children are guarded from diphtheria by what a Japanese and a German did; they are protected from smallpox by an Englishman's work; they are saved from rabies by a Frenchman; they are cured from pellagra through the researches of an Austrian. From birth to death they are surrounded by an invisible host. . . ."[10] Mr. Fosdick saw science, which knew no national frontiers, as drawing men together on the strength of a common task and a more or less universal vocabulary. Add to that the imperative of modernization which dominates policies and priorities in the new nations and opportunities for scientific cooperation are legion as we look to the future.

National and international programs are responding to the challenge through centering attention on regional science centers. The AID is pursuing this objective in Thailand, Turkey, Korea, India and Chile. Its stress is on agriculture, engineering, social and economic planning and

10. Rockefeller Foundation Annual Report, 1944, pp. 9–10.

medicine and public health. The goal is the building of a few strong centers staffed by nationals from the region which would serve the needs for research and training in a broader area. UNESCO, which was among the first of the international organizations to emphasize elementary education and literacy programs, has come to recognize that "without science and technology the horrors of primitivism cannot be dispelled."[11] Bilateral programs involving the Germans, Scandinavians, Canadians, British and Israelis are contributing significantly in Africa and Asia. The same report called attention to a certain imbalance that favors the "hard sciences" and urged "particular applications of the social sciences." Noted for emphasis were "research into population problems, studies of the process of change, and of the best ways to spread new techniques and information in agriculture."[12] The suggestion was made that an organization for the social sciences similar to the International Council of Scientific Unions (ICSU) be founded.

The requirements of science centers cannot be programmed with precision for the many and diverse branches of science. Each science has its peculiar needs. In Marianne Moore's pungent phrase: "Ecstasy affords the occasion and expediency determines the form." Yet a few guidelines can be garnered from the lessons of relatively successful efforts. First, science requires a climate friendly to free and unfettered inquiry. Unfortunately, not every country today or in the future affords such a setting. Second, continuity of staff and support are essential. Publicly financed projects subject to annual appropriations and review are most vulnerable in this respect. Third, developing societies are prone to seek the early payoff, yet any science center deserving of the name must foster both basic and applied research. Fourth, nationalism remains the most powerful force in wide areas of the world. The compulsions of national security and self-sufficiency in time of war and peace drive countries, that by any objective measure lack the resources, to eschew regional cooperation and erect national science centers. A case in point is the drive of Kenya and Tanzania to create their own Medical Schools alongside that of

11. *The United States and UNESCO: Challenges for the Future*, 1966, p. 7.
12. *Ibid.*, p. 9.

Makerere College in Uganda despite common membership in the University of East Africa. Fifth, and a corollary, science centers like universities in general cannot escape the iron laws of economics. They must be fashioned in terms of projected national incomes however strong the pressures to match or outstrip one's neighbors. Well-intentioned donor agencies are as likely to overlook this requirement as are aspiring national leaders.

Fortunately, there are present science centers and others still planned whose records and experiences bear on the future. The International Rice Research Institute established through the good offices of the Ford and Rockefeller Foundations at Los Banos in the Philippines represents a major effort at bringing together in one place worldwide knowledge on rice production. The goal of the Institute is to provide the means of increasing rice yields throughout Asia. Its staff is primarily Asian, recruited with great care by Dr. Robert Chandler of the Rockefeller Foundation. Its varieties have been tested in laboratories and in the field with infinite patience and attention to conditions of soil, climate and topography. One of the varieties has already won worldwide acclaim as IR–8 (the so-called "Miracle Rice") for its dramatic yield capacity. This and other varieties are being tested, cross-bred and adapted in India, Thailand, and other Asian countries. The gulf between the agricultural scientist and the farmer or peasant remains great but the first results are notably encouraging. The lesson to be drawn is that a strong science center can be an invaluable resource both in advancing knowledge and in providing new materials to the peasants and farmers of Asia.

Similar scientific ventures under comparable auspices exist in Mexico and Colombia for corn, wheat and legumes. Significant advances are being made that promise to improve the lot of farmers and the economy in these regions. Both the International Maize and Wheat Improvement Center in Mexico, and the International Center of Tropical Agriculture in Colombia give evidence of transforming the possibilities of yields in these crops for Latin and Central America and for countries in Asia and the Middle East. An Institute of Tropical Agriculture in Nigeria organized and administered by The Ford Foundation with the cooperation of the staff of the Rockefeller Foundation is progressing through the initial stages of its development despite the political conflicts that have wracked that country. Another activity in Nigeria that holds promise for the future is the so-called Ibarapa Project, consisting of the Igbo-Ora Health Center and an associated University of Ibadan medical students' campus. In addition to providing clinical services to surrounding communities, it is an important research center for gathering data on a great variety of rural health problems, and serves to train medical students oriented toward community health and social and preventive medicine. So important are these fields in Nigeria that all medical students at the University are required to spend two months in residence at the center. Summer courses in tropical medicine attract students from abroad and plans are underway for expanding this aspect of the program in the future. A comparable effort with somewhat greater stress on research is the virology program at the University of Ibadan staffed by three members of the world wide virology field staff of the Rockefeller Foundation, who are proceeding with research on the arbo-viruses. Particular emphasis has been placed on tick-borne viruses which are thought to be an important factor in livestock losses in West Africa.

In Asia, an example of an emerging science center is the research and training center at the Faculty of Medical Sciences in Bangkok, Thailand. The center is conceived of as providing an alternative to foreign training in the West for scientific and medical leaders from all of Southeast Asia. The government of Thailand in 1967 appropriated two million dollars toward the costs of new facilities in central Bangkok for this imaginative program. The faculty, with strong support from visiting professors recruited in the United States and Britain, twelve of whom have been assigned by the Rockefeller Foundation, have organized a plan of undergraduate and graduate training culminating in the doctoral degree for basic and medical sciences students. Graduate students will learn by participating in ongoing research of an international standard organized and directed by foreign professors.

The goal throughout will be to train national scientists who in university and industrial settings will carry on their studies once the visiting scholars have left. One underlying principle which is common to the major science programs is the bringing together in one place of the human and scientific resources necessary for serious work. In other words, those who organize such centers give primary attention to having in one place that critical mass of scientists and equipment required for the pursuit of modern science in research and training. For this reason, the numbers of visiting scientists may be greater than is the case with university development programs where one scholar can have a major influence on a broad area or discipline.

### The study of emerging problems

A third approach to the building of indigenous centers is one in which specific problems involving food production, economic planning, population problems and public health are made the basis for new institutions. There is obvious overlap and duplication between the building of science centers and centers for the study of specific problems, and the separation of these two forms of institution building may raise as many questions as it resolves. Obviously centers in community health and social medicine such as the Ibarapa Project in Nigeria fall under both headings. Nevertheless, it is possible to single out those overseas cultural and scientific activities which are aimed at the study and amelioration of particular community problems. An example to illustrate this approach can be drawn from the various community oriented programs in disease prevention, medical care and family planning carried on by the Division of Health Sciences of the Universidad del Valle, in Cali, Colombia. In these activities, the Health Sciences faculty, drawn from the schools of Medicine, Nursing and Rural Health centers, as well as the facilities of the university hospital, have been mobilized to collect data and plan a course of action. The organizing principle on which specific activities are based is the identification of crucial problems for which adequate data or practical solutions may be lacking. The people of Colombia had long felt the need for better data on family practices, health needs and rural-urban problems in the Cauca Valley. The constituent faculty of the Division of Health Sciences has undertaken to provide such basic data through ongoing research and study.

Other examples of problem-oriented work are the various crop programs which have been undertaken in Latin America and Asia. The urgent need in most of the developing countries is for increased agricultural production in the basic crops essential to the economy. Priority is being given to efforts to improve a nation's capacity to increase yields in basic foodstuffs rather than desirable but nonessential products. An example of the dividends of a concerted effort intended to raise yields in the primary crops is the effort in Mexico beginning in 1943 to increase the production of corn, wheat and potatoes. The result of this effort has been to alter Mexico's position in the world food market, particularly in the food grains, from a crop deficit to a crop surplus country. A similar approach has more recently been launched in efforts to increase yields in rice, corn and sorghum in Thailand. Scientists from the United States assigned to the Ministry of Agriculture and Kasetsart University have undertaken in a major effort to substantially increase production. A headquarters base has been provided at Kasetsart University in Bangkok with a major upland research center at Suwan, approximately one hundred and eighty miles northeast of Bangkok. Cooperative work on upland crops is being carried out at four stations; eighteen additional stations operated by the Rice Department are in use. The Departments of Rice and Agriculture of the Ministry of Agriculture and Kasetsart University are pooling their resources and working together in these cooperative projects. These local agencies are providing most of the local costs with external aid going toward staff support, imported equipment, training programs and linkage with related projects in other Asian countries.

Within the framework of university development efforts, projects aimed at increasing food production have also been launched. An example is the expanded effort of the Faculty of Agriculture at Makerere College in Uganda to reorient its research and training toward an emphasis on food production. New departments have been established for Crop Science and Production, Agricultural Engineering and Land Planning, Agricultural Chemistry and Rural Economics and Extension. Greater attention is being given to small tractor development, food crop processing and preservation, tillage techniques, crop protection, dairy cattle feeding and management and the improvement of sweet potatoes, pulses and vegetables.

A similar approach to problem-oriented work has been followed in the field of economics. The Economic Research Bureau of University College Dar es Salaam in Tanzania has evolved a program of research in close cooperation with various ministries of the government of Tanzania. In pursuing its policy-oriented research the Bureau, with a full staff complement of twelve economists, has sought the advice and assistance of government and business agencies in shaping its research efforts. As a result, the agenda for research of this Bureau includes projects and publications dealing with education and educational planning in Tanzania, the balance of payments, monetary policy and rural development. A close working relationship has evolved, making the research of this university bureau "operationally relevant" to the needs of Tanzania.

A similar approach has been followed by the social sciences division of the Institute for Development Studies at University College Nairobi, the Economic Development Research Project of Makerere College, and the Institute for Social Research in Kampala, Uganda. The work of these institutes has been geared to the development needs of the governments of Kenya and Uganda. The list of individual research studies includes the sugar industries in East Africa, the relation of taxation to development, and factors affecting employment. Economists at work in these centers have, through their studies, built up a composite picture of the total economy and its problems with increasing significance for overall economic and social planning.

As pressures mount for limiting the resources available to studies having only remote connections with ongoing development projects, the work of these problem-oriented centers can help to validate the relevance of university work to the needs of new societies. They can help to demonstrate the role of universities in nation-building and resource development.

### Cultural institutions and the humanities

It would be tragic if the new nations in moving into the modern era were "to gain the world and lose their soul." The dilemma they face is that in gaining the benefits of the twentieth century, they seek to preserve the irreplaceable values of indigenous cultures. In the words of a recent report, "It is not just the monuments of history that should concern us, but humbler artifacts as well. The virtual extinction of the Japanese teahouse diminishes the joys of the world."[13] Perhaps the central problem of preserving cultural traditions is the many and varied character of cultural institutions. Archives, museums, native arts and crafts, libraries, historic buildings, natural resources, literature, paintings, sculpture, and the natural environment are all part of culture. So are the great works of politics, philosophy and religion. In order to understand man in society, it is essential to understand his cultural heritage. To do this, men must be as vigilant to the building and strengthening of institutions and opportunities in this realm as in support for science and education.

The practical turn of mind that spells success in modernization often appears less hospitable to the preservation of cultural traditions and monuments. Moreover, relatively few external agencies give culture first priority. All too often comparisons with food production or population control are made at the expense of culture. Yet if "war begins in the minds of men," it is in the works of the human spirit that a healthy and stable society takes root. There are good and bad ideas of government, public responsibility, the common good and the good life that are preserved in literary traditions and a people's cultural legacy. The West has no monopoly of moral philosophy and political wisdom. Our failures in the cultural area have a double aspect. Not only has the United States been negligent in exporting the best of our cultural tradition, settling too often for western movies, but beyond this, "we must learn as well as teach, and to learn the most from the developing countries, we must read more of their books, meet more of their people and see more of their art, drama and dance."[14] There is mutual benefit in sharing the rich legacies that have come down through the ages in every nation's history. "To encourage greater exchange among cultures, UNESCO could

13. UNESCO, *op. cit.*, p. 9.
14. UNESCO, *op. cit.*, p. 10.

make available more translations of literature now available only in languages in limited use, and work to reduce the postage rates between nations in order to stimulate a greater flow of literary and scholarly materials."[15] Agencies like the American Association of University Presses have made valuable contributions. Indigenous regional bodies like the Fondo de Cultura Economica have published inexpensive versions of important writings from North and South America; Franklin Publications have done the same for the Middle East and Africa. The cultural restorations that were assisted by American philanthropy decades ago in Greece and Italy bequeathed a priceless heritage open to the world.

All nations and all peoples need a center for national life, and culture can provide this in the most meaningful ways. National self-conciousness harks back to culture. Respect for enduring traditions and values enables self-confident nations to look to the future for common values that unite rather than divide. Strong cultural institutions can foster fresh understanding of peoples for one another who might otherwise see themselves as dispersed and alone in history.

## OPPORTUNITIES AND RECURRENT PROBLEMS

### Lessons from the private sector

In culture and education, there are lessons to be learned from organizations that have long engaged in technical assistance in this area.

By contrast with far-ranging public activities, experience confirms the wisdom of a private foundation limiting its assistance to a relatively few universities in the developing countries. The extent of its resources and the nature of its experience justify this approach. Through concentrating foundation efforts, the prospect is enhanced for working together in a spirit of mutual confidence with the institutions' top leadership. Visiting scholars whose service to overseas universities is made possible by the foundation can tap the accumulated knowledge of their predecessors and of

15. *Ibid.*

foundation officers. They can reassure themselves that any contribution they make will be central rather than peripheral to the development of their respective fields of knowledge. It is as professors, not advisers, that they are called to serve. They are seen not as "intellectual adventurers" intruding on local academic programs, but as participants invited to join in carrying forward established studies or developing future curricula. One lesson that comes through from every university center at which help has been given is the importance of the visitor's natural functioning as a member of the particular scholarly community. He becomes an accepted and integral part of the faculty, working within and not outside it. Because he is practising the profession for which his credentials and experience best qualify him, he runs less risk of being seen as an alien force in a major national enterprise—education.

As the university development program moved ahead, requests for assistance in other spheres have multiplied. Since the goal from the beginning has been the strengthing of institutions as a whole, the need for reinforcing basic structures becomes self-evident. The fiscal and administrative infrastructure, although less visible, is as basic as the academic superstructure. Yet here it is easier to identify needs than to provide answers. A professor in physics or economics functions in broadly similar terms in any university. There are, of course, needs for new teaching materials and a syllabus organically linked with cultural patterns and evolving social and educational institutions. The best theoretical and descriptive writings must be adapted to changing local circumstances. At the center of the basic disciplines, whether in the physical or social sciences, is a hard core of concepts and principles to be taught. This seems less clear of fiscal and administrative practices especially when they are the outgrowth of different national or colonial traditions operating overtime. The work of a registrar or estates officer in an African university is not the same as someone responsible for business management elsewhere. The flow of matters requiring action to the desk of the Vice Chancellor may not be equal or similar in kind to that reaching a university president. Efficiency and fiscal studies are useful but many overseas institutions continue to look for more relevant types of surveys and better guidance on their implementation.

A few general principles, then, are illustrative of the lessons that derive from experience in the private sector. First, concentration is essential to assure the form and quality of assistance required. Obviously, foundations in particular lack the resources to scatter their assistance everywhere. Even governmental aid is limited. For a recipient to benefit significantly, a certain critical mass of help is required whether it takes the form of human or material resources or capital. The leadership of developing institutions is quick to measure the extent of commitment of cooperating bodies. Comparisons are made between visitors who come to stay and those who never unpack their bags. Full and frank exchange of ideas is the result, not the forerunner, of mutual commitment. Yet intimate, unguarded and self-critical discussion is vital if assistance is to make a difference. To mold a partnership in institution building is to build a framework within which consultation goes on and mutually acceptable, far-reaching decisions are made. By contrast, casual involvement in institutional development leaves to hit and run those actions that shape the future. Whether the subject is the selection of a fellow, reworking the syllabus, or planning a new curriculum, the partners are engaged in what is ultimately the institution's most serious business. Whether they succeed or fail depends on whether these topics are considered casually en route to the airport or through the solemn and deliberate processes of ongoing institutional life.

A corollary of the concentration principle stems from the weight of responsibility it throws on local leadership and national sponsors. In the same way that not every nation has made the hard decisions prerequisite to foreign assistance, not every institution has prepared itself for genuine organic growth. It may have failed to come forward with a practical design for upgrading its faculty or neglected research opportunities or overlooked salary problems or forgotten about community support. Or what may be lacking is a nucleus of devoted and responsible leaders willing and able to foster institutional growth if necessary at the expense of their own professional advancement and prestige. There are certain matters that institutions, no less than individuals or nations, cannot leave to chance. What is to be their role in a wider geographic region? How are they to weight mass growth in relation to the pursuit of excellence? How much or how little should they undertake in a specific field? Is their mission to train the teachers, public servants, engineers and doctors to serve the nation and other social and educational institutions? Or is their role conceived in more parochial though worthy terms of building a civic culture for their immediate constituents? Finally, has the leadership made a fresh and self-critical review of strengths and weaknesses and laid down the broad guidelines for responding to institutional needs? Recognizing that its resources are always more restricted than its needs, how far has it gone in establishing priorities for determining points of emphasis next year or three or five years hence?

Partners in institution building who can at best assist only a few well-qualified institutions cannot escape the obligation to assess the many factors essential to growth. Perhaps what is needed is an institutional equivalent of the pilot's check list for review before clearing the aircraft for flight. But at the end of the day when the many factors essential to growth have been considered, partners must return to consider the institution as a whole. For whether the aim is university development or building a strong and vital research institute, the organization is somehow more than the sum of its parts. Those who assess in order to help must acquire the knack of measuring the potential and strength of institutions in the process of evolving. Universities in some parts of the world are little more than loose collections of faculties. If it is the university that invites development, this fact may lead to exclusion. Or it may require a new approach to institution building. If outside donor organizations concentrate their resources at a few developing institutions, the corollary of their assistance is single-minded concentration by the leadership on the central problems of institution building.

A second principle that we can glean from the broad range of private assistance underscores the importance of identifying and defining discrete and manageable areas of assistance. This need is an outgrowth of the nature of technical assistance. Outside help is inevitably marginal help. At the peak of the Marshall Plan, the flow of aid never exceeded four per cent of Europe's capital needs. Private foundations in particular must come to a judicious determination on the focus of their aid. Policies follow questions that go to the heart of cooperative efforts. What are the recipient country's most urgent and pressing needs and what is it doing about them? What is it doing for itself and what does it seek from others? Viewed realistically, what capacity does the donor agency possess, or can it acquire, for assistance in those areas likely to make a genuine difference? Whether the choice is agriculture or virus research or improving an economics faculty, there are dividends of defining and identifying areas of need and matching them against available outside resources. In Thailand, the Rockefeller Foundation has concentrated its efforts to assist university development by focusing on the strengthening of three basic disciplines: the basic sciences centering around biochemistry, agriculture and economics. Within its operating agricultural programs, the emphasis has been on research and training programs directed toward strengthening a country's ability to produce certain basic food crops such as corn, wheat, sorghum, potatoes and rice. Crops have been chosen because they were crucial for specific economies. Thus corn and wheat have been the focus in Mexico and rice and sorghum in Asia. The goal has been improved varieties and techniques not across the entire agricultural spectrum but in areas where need and capacity could be joined. Again in the Foundation's university development efforts, its focus has been on disciplines ready and able to use assistance for which the sources of intellectual cooperation were in sight.

A third principle already adumbrated is the vital importance of continuity. The Rockefeller Foundation's Mexican Agriculture Program was inaugurated in 1943. It has evolved through the stage of assistance to a national program carefully housed in the Office of Special Studies within the Ministry of Agriculture to the current International Corn and Wheat Program. More than twenty years later, a handful of the original team of Rockefeller Foundation agricultural scientists continue to serve as participant advisors in a fully Mexican international agricultural program aiming to share with others accumulated knowledge developed over the past two decades. Similarly, the University of the Philippines under the vital and dynamic leadership of General Carlos P. Romulo has reached the stage, particularly in the Arts and Sciences, where strategically placed assistance can enable it to move to a new level of excellence. How shortsighted it would be for agencies that had faithfully provided fellowship help in other less hopeful eras to terminate abruptly all forms of aid.

Finally, a career service of men engaged in assistance to developing institutions is essential. The Gardner Report proposes an AID Career Service backstopped by a cadre of AID reservists. Experiences that hark back to the International Health Division of the Rockefeller Foundation point the way to the maintenance of professional competence for international service. If Henry Wriston is right when he states that, "first-class problems attract first-class minds," the rallying of qualified personnel should not be impossible. The Rockefeller Foundation in its University Development Program has been encouraged by the interest of first-rate scholars in serving abroad as visiting professors, heads of departments and even deans. Some have been recruited as regular Foundation staff, others as temporary personnel and others as scholars on leave from their own universities. A career service for university development must be flexible enough to provide for commitments ranging across a sliding scale of interest. Some will be engaged more or less permanently and others for a year or two. It is obvious that any plan for a career service that would attract the best minds must allow for both research and service—the continuation of a scholar's most deeply cherished scientific interests. Essential will be the presence in any organized effort at a university development center of at least a few topflight leaders devoting themselves full-time to academic administration and teaching. Their presence at the heart of the development enterprise leaves room for researchers who teach by carrying forward their inquiries.

In the end, the fate of American education abroad is dependent on responsible and well-qualified people engaged in tasks for which there is recognized need. Sometimes this involves doing well what a scholar is required to do in any educational setting. Other times the adaptation must be more drastic. Perhaps the success of the American educational effort is greatest when the approach is indirect and oblique. It may be that American agronomists, economists or virologists contribute most when they labor as scientists and scholars drawing on the full range of knowledge which they can appropriate, not because they are Americans but because of professional competence. If this is the test of American education, it will more likely be realized within the framework of an organized, concentrated, career-oriented approach to institution building abroad.

### The problem of national sensitivity

The March 29, 1967 statement of the Trustees of Education and World Affairs begins with the sentence: "The overseas interests and activities of U.S. education have now come under renewed public discussion as a consequence of the disclosures of CIA financing of various private groups." The genius of cultural exchange in the private sector has been its relative independence of political and ideological controls. Freedom of cultural agencies to operate from the principle of "the packed suitcase," eschewing influence or domination by any political authority, has been a source of strength. With the mounting weight of public financing, the line of independence has been more difficult to maintain, in appearance if not in fact. As Americans are at work in foreign areas where aspiring political groups are ready and alert to exploit evidence, real or imagined, of American power in their midst, restraint and judgment are vital in the conduct of cultural activities.

In response to this challenge, the Trustees of Education and World Affairs have offered the following guidelines as a framework of operations for all American institutions and agencies abroad:

1. "The universities must assume an active and effective role in providing safeguards and setting high standards for U.S. study and research undertakings overseas." Far from lowering levels of personal responsibility and professional integrity abroad, Americans engaged in this important task must dedicate themselves anew to the highest standards of which they are capable.

2. "The university must take the lead in insisting on the

rule of candor and full disclosure in connection with all overseas research." This sets limits to the tasks scholars may undertake. It rules out certain types of activities that may be possible within scientific laboratories in the United States.

3. "The university should reject covert funding of overseas research and at the same time press for an enlargement in the grant-making capacity of those government agencies which are not part of the military and intelligence complexes." At the same time, we should remember that worthwhile programs that start modestly and "grow big" are more likely to be successful.

4. "The university should use all available means to assure that suitable academic quality standards are met with respect to overseas research projects and the scholars who will carry them out." It has unfortunately been the case that respected institutions have farmed out overseas projects while keeping intact at home the corps of their most qualified scholars. Overseas activities test the mettle of our best minds and leaders. We cannot afford to entrust this vital task to second-class educators and scholars.

5. "The university should seek to assure that the overseas research of its faculty members enhances the American academic presence abroad . . . It can do so partly by encouraging its scholars . . . to take active account of the other country's developmental needs in education and research." In short, scholars going abroad should be enjoined to engage in institution building.

6. "The university should lend its support to the strengthening of our educational representation abroad as a basis for more effective cooperation with the academic communities of other countries." The recruitment and appointment of first-class educators as Education Officers in our embassies offers one hopeful avenue of progress, but thus far embarrassingly little progress has been made in pursuing this objective.

7. "Through its graduate faculties and professional schools, the university should begin to build into the training of students an appreciation of the types of problems that are involved in overseas research." Since World War II, we have accumulated a substantial body of experience in over-

seas work and ways must be found to transmit this to students and future leaders.

## Perspectives on the future

Americans have a penchant for stressing their failures and giving short shrift to successes. Nowhere is this more apparent than in international relations. On the war-peace front, this leads us to obscure the fact that there has been no general war for more than two decades—a tribute to the steady resolve and cool nerves of our policy-makers. In cultural relations, achievements are even more conspicuous and this in the face of the sudden and unforeseen responsibilities dedicated Americans have assumed around the globe. We have assisted friendly nations in building more stable economies, meeting severe problems of food deficits, training indigenous leadership, staffing public services and scientific establishments, building stronger educational institutions, stabilizing population growth and facing a broad range of social and economic problems. In a time of increasing pressures and rising tensions at home, Americans understandably are tempted to "rest on their oars." Twenty years of foreign assistance which have brought notable success have of course produced few miracles, any more than hard labor at home has solved all our national problems. A winter of discontent was bound to set in. A full and discerning perspective of the future requires that we see our responsibilities "steady and see them whole."

The burdens and challenges we have taken up with courage and determination have brought us closer to the goal of a better world. But vast and unresolved issues remain. Per capita income in the developing countries hovers between $50 and $100 compared with a figure in this country substantially greater than $3000. We have scores of colleges and universities that surpass in material and intellectual endowments the best national institutions in the developing countries. Leadership remains in short supply in almost every sector. Teachers, doctors, engineers and agriculturalists are too few and too concentrated in urban areas. New professions are required such as para-medical specialists. Scientists and professors must move out of their laboratories and classrooms if urgent needs are to be resolved. Americans schooled in the land-grant college tradition and in other traditions of service have much to offer foreign educators. Innovations that lead to the creation of an "international faculty" within strong American universities would contribute much.

We have received the torch from others who have brought the benefits of culture and civilization to the world. We must not abandon our course in mid-passage; the task is only partly completed. There is need for fresh thinking and renewed energy, but history will hold us accountable if we drop the torch. More than we know, Americans will be tested and judged by our view of the future and the quality of our response.

# Notes on the Contributors

PAUL J. BRAISTED is president of The Hazen Foundation. He has been a member of UNESCO's international advisory committee on the Major Project concerned with the Mutual Appreciation of Asian and Western Cultural Values, and member of the U.S. National Commission on UNESCO.

GEORGE N. SHUSTER, president emeritus of Hunter College, is United States representative to the executive board of UNESCO and assistant to the president of Notre Dame University. He has been chairman of the Institute of International Education and a member of the general advisory committee to the Division of Cultural Relations, the State Department. Dr. Shuster has written numerous books on education, the latest being *The Ground I Walked On.*

W. McNEIL LOWRY is a vice president of The Ford Foundation. He has been director of the Foundation's Program in Humanities and the Arts. He helped to found and edit *Accent,* a quarterly of new literature, and was at one time chief of the Washington Bureau of the Cox Newspapers.

GERTRUDE S. HOOKER is visiting professor of Comparative Literature at The University of Hartford. In 1961–65 she was on the staff of The Ford Foundation in Humanities and the Arts. From 1951–61 Dr. Hooker was a cultural officer in Rome and Paris, and from 1945–50, an editor of *Common Cause—a Journal of One World.*

C. EASTON ROTHWELL is president emeritus of Mills College. Author and professor of history, Dr. Rothwell was director of the Hoover Institute and Library, 1952–59, and is currently consultant on education in Asia to the Asia Foundation.

ROGER REVELLE is director of the Harvard Center for Population Studies. He is a former director of the Scripps Institution of Oceanography and science advisor to the Secretary of the Interior. Dr. Revelle has been head of the Geophysics Branch, Office of Naval Research; member of the United States Commission for UNESCO and of panels of the President's Science Advisory Committee.

KENNETH W. THOMPSON is vice president of the Rockefeller Foundation. Formerly a university professor in social science, Dr. Thompson is author of numerous books on foreign policy and international affairs, the latest being *Foreign Policies in a World Of Change*.

# Index

205

# The American Assembly

The American Assembly holds meetings of national leaders and publishes books to illuminate issues of United States policy. The Assembly is a national, non-partisan educational institution, incorporated in the State of New York.

The Trustees of the Assembly approve a topic for presentation in a background book, authoritatively designed and written to aid deliberations at national Assembly sessions at Arden House, the Harriman Campus of Columbia University. These books are also used to support discussion at regional Assembly sessions and to evoke consideration by the general public.

All sessions of the Assembly, whether international, national or local, issue and publicize independent reports of conclusions and recommendations on the topic at hand. Participants in these sessions constitute a wide range of experience and competence.

American Assembly books are purchased and put to use by thousands of individuals, libraries, businesses, public agencies, nongovernmental organizations, educational institutions, discussion meetings and service groups. Since 1960 Assembly books have been published by Prentice-Hall, Inc., Frederick A. Praeger, Inc., and Columbia Books. The subjects of Assembly studies to date are:

1951—UNITED STATES-WESTERN EUROPE
        RELATIONSHIPS
1952—INFLATION
1953—ECONOMIC SECURITY FOR AMERICANS
1954—THE UNITED STATES STAKE IN THE
        UNITED NATIONS
    —THE FEDERAL GOVERNMENT SERVICE
1955—UNITED STATES AGRICULTURE
    —THE FORTY-EIGHT STATES

—OMBUDSMEN FOR AMERICAN
GOVERNMENT?
1968—LAW IN A CHANGING AMERICA
—THE USES OF THE SEAS
—WORLD HUNGER

Second Editions:

1962—THE UNITED STATES AND THE FAR EAST
1963—THE UNITED STATES AND LATIN
AMERICA
—THE UNITED STATES AND AFRICA
1964—UNITED STATES MONETARY POLICY
1965—THE FEDERAL GOVERNMENT SERVICE
—THE REPRESENTATION OF THE UNITED
STATES ABROAD
1968—OUTER SPACE: PROSPECTS FOR MAN AND
SOCIETY
—CULTURAL AFFAIRS AND FOREIGN
RELATIONS

# The American Assembly

211